Five Gateways
Our Journey of Ascension

by

Chris Bourne
Openhand Foundation

Five Gateways
by Chris Bourne, Openhand Foundation

First Edition printed 5th May 2010
Published by Openhand Press

Copyright Openhand Foundation 2010
www.openhandweb.org

ISBN 978-0-9556792-0-9

Cover design: Stephie Shoebridge

for all my brothers and sisters...

"Be a lamp unto yourself.
Don't search for light anywhere else;
the light is already there, the fire is already there.
Just probe a little deeper into your being, enquire.
Maybe much ash has gathered around the fire...
Just probe deep inside, and you will find the spark again.
And once you have found a single spark inside you,
you will become a flame, soon you will be a fire...
a fire that purifies, a fire that transforms,
a fire that gives you a new birth and a new being.
Be a lamp unto yourself."

Last words of Gautama, the Buddha

Contents

Glossary

Terms commonly used in this book are listed below...

Ascension: when a sentient life form moves from one vibrational state of existence to the next higher one.

Attachment: when a soul becomes identified with the external 'drama' in some particular way.

Bodily vehicles of expression: the human bodily vehicles formed from Separation Consciousness (collectively termed the "bodymind") through which the soul expresses.

The seven bodily vehicles are outlined here...

Spirit light body: facilitates multidimensional experience. Also known as the "merkaba" (connected via the crown chakra).

Celestial body: holds, stimulates and reflects authentic recognition of our soul (connected via the third eye).

Higher mind: harmonises with the divine flow and manifests the conditions for "Right Action" aligned with the universe (connected via the throat chakra).

Causal body: (the energy body) retains karma - the blue print for each incarnation (connected via the heart chakra).

Subconscious mind: interprets abstract wisdom of higher mind and facilitates our psychic skills in a third dimensional way (connected via the solar plexus chakra).

Emotional body: holds, processes and expresses our emotional state (connected via the sacral chakra).

Physical Body: the sum collection of consciousness cells forming the physical body (connected via the base chakra).

Chakra: an etheric location within a human being where Soul Consciousness infuses into the bodily vehicles of expression.

The seven main chakras are outlined below...

Base chakra: the etheric centre where Soul Consciousness infuses into the physical body. Positioned at the coccyx and also known as the "root chakra".

Sacral chakra: the etheric centre where Soul Consciousness infuses into the emotional body. Positioned roughly where the spine and pelvis meet.

Solar plexus chakra: the etheric centre infusing Soul Consciousness into the subconscious mind.

Heart chakra: where Soul Consciousness infuses into the causal body. Based on the spine at the general level of the heart.

Throat chakra: the etheric centre where Soul Consciousness infuses into the "higher mind" bodily vehicle of expression.

Third eye: the general centre of consciousness for the soul within a human being. Located in the centre of the head at the pineal gland. Also known as "the soul centre".

Crown chakra: the etheric centre where Soul Consciousness infuses into the spirit light body.

Consciousness: awareness or presence - life itself.

The key consciousness terms used in this book are as follows...

Benevolent Consciousness: a benevolent life form assisting in the natural evolutionary process of another life form. Also frequently referred to as "Higher Guiding Consciousness".

Opposing Consciousness: a non benevolent life form opposing the natural evolutionary process of another for its own benefit.

Separation Consciousness: consciousness generating the illusion of separation between sentient life forms.

Unity Consciousness: consciousness connecting all sentient life forms and drawing them back to ever higher degrees of unity.

Consciousness landscape: an interconnected pattern of information held within our consciousness and formed by observing external signs and symbols. When lightly held and referenced within the bodymind, it forms the landscape through which the soul flows.

Distorted behaviour patterns: conditioned behaviour patterns formed from fixed neural pathways in the brain caused by an attachment of the soul to the external drama. They are generated in educational environments e.g. parents, schools, careers and generally accepted social/political/religious/scientific attitudes within society.

Dimension: something which defines a particular vibrational location in the universe.

Dimensional realm: a grouping of dimensions forming one plane of existence - for example the 'Third Dimensional Realm' where we currently exist (sometimes mistakenly called a "parallel universe").

Divine Purpose: the naturally benevolent and compassionate shaping purpose of the universe bringing sentient life to perfection.

Earth bound soul: a soul that has left the body and yet remains in the Third Dimensional Realm due to over attachment to this plane.

Enlightened state: when a sentient life form is experiencing itself as what it truly is - the Seer - non-identified presence.

Enlightenment: when a sentient life form is constantly experiencing itself as the Seer.

Ego: where the soul has formed an identity with the bodymind.

Gateways of Light: transition points from one level or state of consciousness to a higher more expanded one.

The five key expansions of consciousness are outlined below...

Awakening: we awaken to the magic of the soul and our interconnectedness with all life.

Realignment: we surrender to the supreme governance of the soul in our lives. We align with the Divine Purpose.

Transfiguration: where we make the dramatic shift of perception from identification with the personality to being the Seer expressed as the soul through the bodymind.

Enlightenment: where final 'fragments' of the soul still identifying with the personality are released and 'reconnected'. The soul becomes fully integral within our being.

Resurrection: where our seven bodily vehicles of expression are finally cleansed, reactivated and re-energised. The soul unfolds into multidimensional living.

Identity: when the soul builds a web of conditioned behaviours (fixed neural pathways) within the brain and identifies with them - the soul is attached to the ego (personality).

    The key identities referred to in this book are listed below...

    Inner child identity: a complex web of fixed neural pathways forming in early childhood.

    Inner teenager identity: a complex web of fixed neural pathways forming at or shortly after puberty.

    Shadow identity: a 'fragment' of the soul identifying with karma. Also known as the "shadow".

Karma: an attachment formed by the soul to a particular experience in a past life which then regenerates a similar experience in the current incarnation in order to release the attachment.

Right Action: action which is at one with the natural directional flow of the universe as a whole.

Right Outcome: when Right Action is made manifest.

Sentient life form: a separate, identifiable life form.

Soul: a unique expression of the Seer animating a sentient life form.

Soul family: a group of closely related souls all vibrating on a similarly aligned harmonic and assisting each other in their spiritual evolution.

Synchronicity: when seemingly random occurrences gather together in a definable pattern thereby rendering a deeper meaning or story.

The Matrix: a complex energy web of conditioned behaviours formed from mass human subconsciousness.

The Observer: an aspect of mind - a temporary inner identity - formed from the intention to observe thoughts, emotions, motivations, feelings and behaviours.

The Heart Centre: a more expanded evolution of the Observer. The place where we feel and surrender to the natural pull of our soul.

The Seer: non-identified presence - the one being from which all life is formed. Also referred to as "pure presence", "The Absolute", "The True Self" and "God".

The Source: the point of singularity before this universe arose. It is also referred to as "Unity" and also the "Source of All Life".

Prologue

"There will come a time when you believe everything is finished. That will be the beginning."

Louis L'Amour

The Message

For forty years of my life, I had lived in darkness. I had been cast adrift in the virtual prison we call the mind. Just like many across our planet today, I was consumed within society's ultimate deception: the delusion that we are all separate from one another; that we have to fight and struggle in life to get what we want; that there is no benevolent guiding hand leading us to our ultimate salvation. Then suddenly, out of the blue, this veil of deceit was, for me, forever shattered.

Through a sequence of miraculous experiences, I was fully awakened to our absolute authentic reality. A universal orchestra of co-creative activity sang its sweet melody loud and clear. Higher consciousness was speaking to me through the synchronistic pattern of life leading me on a journey of self realisation. Situations, events, circumstances and chance meetings conspired to reveal an inner pathway through consciousness itself. I was taken through five "Gateways of Light" leading to my Enlightenment and Ascension. Frequently painful, sometimes terrifying, it was, and continues to be, a magical journey of unfolding, flowing as one with my soul, experiencing ever finer tastes of universal unity and harmony. In short, I have been reacquainted with our birthright, to know ourselves as what we really are - the unfathomable "Seer" that exists in and through all things.

Through that journey of inner unfolding, I was reconnected with the place of universal knowing, a vast cosmic library of divine energy I have come to know as "Unity Consciousness"; an imperishable flow of unconditional love that we can all gain access to by letting go of the governance of the mind and surrendering into the heart.

In so doing, it has become abundantly clear to me that my purpose here is to bring a message. Not a channelling, it was rather a 'download' of energy which infused directly into my being and became a part of me. Although the message may have originated at a higher source, I now recognise it as my own. So rather than just simply speaking it, I live it and it animates my being.

Initially, it was difficult for me to fully process the message through the veils of distorted human thinking, and even more difficult to put it into words. However, the message would not go away and so I persevered and with the patient help of Benevolent Consciousness, I finally unveiled the truth as a deep inner knowing. Now, after much dedicated soul searching, I am comfortable that I have found the right vocabulary to capture the true essence of it.

I know the message is of vital importance to all humanity at this time of great turmoil and transition. I know in my heart it provides the solution to every single problem we currently face. It is one which has been gifted to us before, but it has been much misunderstood and maligned. Time is running out, we need to dust off the pages of history and look at the message with fresh eyes. We need to open our minds and unlock the hidden code buried in our hearts. So what was the message? It was, and continues to be, this...

"We stand on the brink of a miraculous new evolution for mankind. A higher vibrational reality is beckoning us founded on unconditional love for all life and synchronistic co-creativity; it is a 'heaven' which exists here and now all around us. In this new paradigm, we are completely at one with each other and all life. There is no killing, manipulation, or exploitation of ANY sentient life form or natural resource. All is shared and experienced in harmony without fear. There is absolute trust in our at-one-ment with the divine. Indeed we experience ourselves AS THE DIVINE, not separate from it. Our living purpose is self-realisation and spiritual enrichment.

The new paradigm is already unfolding all around us, but it is difficult to see, taste and feel as the old world values crumble and collapse. All life and all structure is formed from universal life energy - from pure consciousness. Nothing is stationary, the underlying fabric from which all life is woven, is naturally evolving to ever higher states of harmony and at-one-ment. It is a river of life flowing ceaselessly through every single moment and nothing can resist its eternal flow. Anything that is of lower vibration, lower harmony, anything that sustains inequity and the selfish exploitation of life, will over time, literally fall apart.

That is what is happening to our society right now. To many, it is an inequitable and unjust system based on exploitation, fear and greed. It is one that has unceremoniously shunted our existence out of harmony with our planetary system and our universe as a whole. Industrial consumerism, the supposed 'virtuous' building block upon which the very fabric of our society has been founded, is now tumbling. It has become an insatiable beast that has been raping Mother Earth in this realm, stripping her bare of natural resources to fix humanity's ever burgeoning addictions. We have built a society on false promises and written countless blank cheques which can no longer be cashed. We have founded our lives on sand and the tide is now fast coming in.

As this turbulent transition takes place, we are each being invited to join the new paradigm; we each have a ticket for that journey. To get on board, we have to go within, peel away our attachments to the material world, process out our fear based thinking and dissolve distorted behaviour patterns that limit us. It is these that constrict and confine us in the lower level of consciousness. We are being invited to separate out the authentic characteristics of our soul, from the conditioned beliefs, illusionary needs and false agendas that have been programmed within us. We have to let this darkened veil fall from our eyes so that the new world can unfold into view.

So in this eleventh hour, we are each being presented with a choice. Either we continue to buy into the collapsing fear based mentality of division and struggle or we step into the heart and reconnect with our divine birthright. Benevolent Consciousness is drawing ever closer to help those prepared to listen. We are being provided with a route map through the inner landscape. The map guides us through Five Gateways of consciousness leading to our Enlightenment and Ascension into the higher paradigm. It is a process that has been followed by spiritual masters throughout the ages and has the power to unite evolving people everywhere.

We each follow a unique pathway as we ascend the spiritual mountain, but those who have climbed before us report similar experiences, challenges and opportunities as we pass key 'altitudes' on route to the summit. The map is a gift to humanity in these profound times of great change. It offers the priceless opportunity to come to know ourselves experientially as what we truly are - the "Seer" - the eternal Source of all creation. In so doing, we move back into harmony with the natural flow of the universe and unfold the magical lives we were born to live."

Over five years, the message evolved with an experiential explanation of how to tune into higher guidance and what we may experience as we follow our inner journey of Ascension, which I share in this book. It is not an easy journey, there are many external distorting and manipulating influences that would attach us to the external drama of life and thereby divert us from our path. However, if we apply ourselves diligently to the task of unveiling our inherent beingness, then a beautiful adventure of self discovery unfolds before us, full of mystery, miracles and magic.

I know, beyond a shadow of doubt, that success is open to every single one of us who ventures honestly down the path. Are you ready to make that journey? If so, Five Gateways will help guide you on your way.

The Five Gateways
-introduction-

What is Ascension?

Our planetary system is undergoing an entirely natural evolutionary process called "Ascension". In other words, it is moving from a lower vibrational reality to a higher one. It is an underlying flow of energy which is affecting every single thought, emotion and feeling we are currently having. Whether we know it or not, how we process this inner movement of consciousness influences every choice we make and shapes the outer circumstances of our lives. The experiences on the inside, although frequently quite subtle, are nevertheless having a profound and radical effect in our outer world. Our spiritual evolution - our Ascension - is not something we can conveniently sweep under the carpet whilst we get on with the day-job; in every moment, the underlying flow of energy is influencing and shaping our lives in a deeply profound way.

So what is Ascension, what exactly does the term mean? Imagine for one moment the creation of the universe observed as the Big Bang with a radiant explosion of light. We could perhaps imagine ourselves as the "Source" of a universal pond, spontaneously subdividing, causing ripples of consciousness to spread outwards in all directions from the centre. As the waves radiate further outwards, they increase in amplitude, in other words they get bigger. This also increases the width of each wave - their wavelength - which in turn lowers their frequency of vibration. Thus consciousness gets denser; it con-denses into what we experience as matter. Taking our pond analogy deeper, we might consider each wave on the pond represents a "Dimensional Realm" each vibrating at a different frequency. We currently live in the Third Dimensional Realm, a particularly dense vibration at the water's edge quite removed from the Source.

Now on the surface of our imaginary pond, it appears as though the water is flowing outwards - in fact it is only the disturbance of the waves flowing, the water itself moves only up and down. You might consider the water to be held in place by an undertow to counterbalance the outward flow. Again, this phenomenon represents a wonderful analogy for the universe as a whole, where on the surface (in physical time space), it appears as if the universe is spreading outwards to ever greater separation, which we experience as greater disconnection from the Source and therefore greater 'dis-ease'. It is probably this feeling of separation which causes ignorance and the inconsiderate exploitation of other sentient life forms such as Mother Earth for example. Quantum science observes this as an increase in 'dis-order' known as an increase in "positive entropy" meaning the flow from a higher, more harmonious energetic state, to a lower, more scattered one.

However, 'under the surface of the universe' in what we might call "Unity Consciousness space" (quantum science calls it "negative time space"), there is a flow back to the Source to ever greater degrees of order, harmony and ease. We can actually feel this pull when we get out of the mind and into the heart, which guides us in a way that brings increasing inner peace, greater self acceptance, ever expanding joy and at-one-ment with all life. Science refers to this as an "increase in negative entropy" but to me "unconditional love" seems a much more appropriate description!

This flow back to the Source is called Ascension. Specifically, it is where the centre of consciousness of a sentient being is flowing to ever higher vibrational realms of existence. Using our pond analogy, it is moving from one wave at the edge of the pond to continually higher ones closer to the centre. It is a heavenly process which is naturally unfolding for all sentient life forms including "Gaia" - the Soul of the Earth herself. The problem for humanity right now is that our resistance to this process is causing immeasurable pain and suffering from poverty and disease, to isolation, fear and despair.

Why is it then that our society seems not to accept, or even observe, the process of Ascension? Why is it that so many people are resisting the movement to ever higher vibrations of love, harmony and at-one-ment with all life? Why is it that most people do not currently experience this expanded reality which can be sensed and felt in Unity Consciousness space? It is because the physical aspect of the human being which many identify with is only designed to tune into three dimensional reality. We are each bombarded with literally billions of bits of information about our reality every second and yet the average human brain can only process a very tiny proportion of this. To cope with the overload, the brain forms a map of the reality it has come to expect and filters out the rest of the information. Since our outer world is shaped by our inner state of consciousness, then our experience of reality becomes severely limited. In other words, we confine ourselves to what we experience only at the edge of the pond.

However, when we are able to let go of our conditioned thinking and programmed beliefs, then our soul unfolds into other layers of consciousness and we become increasingly able to tune into a much wider array of the available information. We get to experience and taste other dimensional realms of reality beyond this one. This is not theory; people right across our planet today are experiencing many of these other realms. We might consider it like tuning into different stations on the radio. All radio bands exists in the same space and time, but at different frequencies. The problem for humanity right now is that we have become too used to just one frequency, one station on the radio. If we want to experience the full complement of life, we have to tune the dial to get to the higher vibrations.

As we access more of this expanded reality, it often comes with profound joy as we rediscover our interconnectedness with the whole of life. It is then that the next plane of existence - the Fifth Dimensional Realm - comes into view expressed through co-creative synchronicity. In short, the more familiar we become with the guiding patterning of all events, the more it dawns on us that we are not living in one world, but two. The higher plane of existence is overlapping this one. Whilst our day-to-day five-sense experience still resides in the usual physical plane, our psychic and intuitive senses enable us to interpret physical phenomenon as symbolic representations of the higher realm. Some people are already able to centre their consciousness in the new plane and taste the flow of divine oneness and unconditional love that is omnipresent there. Others have profoundly clear visions of this New World (perhaps more appropriately "Renewed World").

This new reality can only be accessed however, when we have found a good degree of inner stillness, which in itself arises from becoming more surrendered and at one with our natural planetary ecosystem. When we do this, then Gaia begins to speak to us, quietly at first, but then as we tune in more consistently, her sweet voice becomes increasingly clear and undeniable. Our consciousness is drawn to the underlying message prevalent in all events and a story begins to unfold before our very eyes. The story is a double sided coin. On the one side, there is the beauty, joy and harmony of the unfolding higher existence and on the other, there is the fear, pain and struggle of the lower reality crumbling around us. The two strongly contrasting stories are happening in the same place at the same time and we have a choice as to which one we buy into.

Currently, society's approach to our problems is one of increasing technical evolution, but increasing human evolution is our natural pathway, unfolding skills and sensitivity many of us probably never dreamed possible. It happens when we surrender and let go of the conditioned reality we have come to expect - the darker side of the coin. As we do so, slowly but surely, we are guided to the higher story - the brighter side. More of the universe unfolds before our eyes or put more appropriately, WE unfold into new realms. We reconnect with our inherent divinity and rediscover ourselves as multidimensional beings.

Within the overall process of Ascension, there is what we might call an "ascending realm shift", where a sentient life form makes a transition from one realm of existence into the next higher one. From my perspective, Mother Earth is now shifting her centre of consciousness into the Fifth Dimension, a process which is due to complete in 2012. So why do we still experience her in this physical plane? It is because she maintains energies here - a super conscious field - a bridge for us to connect with and raise our vibration to the level required to transition across from the old world to the new.

In order to raise our vibration to the required frequency, we must go inwards and 'open up' by acknowledging our genuine feelings and releasing tightness and tension caused by our attachment to the physical drama of life. The more we open and feel the unconditional love, joy and harmony, the more we understand what blockages are limiting our Ascension and how to process them out. As we do so, our vibration rises and we transition through the Five Gateways of inner consciousness - the "Gateways of Light".

So when we have passed through these Gateways, does that mean we automatically leave the physical body? The answer to this question depends entirely on what our purpose here is. Many people are here to assist in the Ascension of others, so we may still remain in physical incarnation in order to help more effectively. Although we still maintain physical presence in the Third Dimension, our soul is centred in the higher reality. In short, we are already ascended.

Mother Earth herself continues to live in the two realms although her centre of consciousness is now centring more in the Fifth Dimension. She is quietly withdrawing her energies ever higher, coaxing more of us 'upwards' across her superconscious bridge. The movement of energy is compassionate and gentle, however because many are still resisting this natural flow, there is a growing polarity between the higher and lower realms, between light and dark. This is why those who are still locked in the old fear based mentality are experiencing increasing doubt, fear and worry as they try to manipulate and control ever dwindling natural resources in the lower realm. This is why anger, frustration and resentment are also on the increase as people struggle for security. Instinctively, they can feel the draining away of energy.

This fear based reality cannot exist indefinitely. That would be to contradict the natural evolutionary process of the universe which has 'breathed out' and is now 'breathing back in' again. Hence we are being guided through the inner layers of consciousness - the Five Gateways - to the next chapter of the human story.

What are the Gateways of Light?
Since my initial awakening, I have been fully engaged in helping others through their own spiritual awakenings. I have witnessed through many real life encounters the reoccurring pattern of the five key expansions of consciousness as people unfold internally. These observations appear to be closely aligned with a number of other contemporary and ancient spiritual teachings. Whilst I consider the evolutionary pathway for each of us to be unique, to me it is clearly consistent, that those ascending tend to pass through these five key 'altitudes' (even though we might not always recognise them).

Many people have found it of profound benefit to have a reasonable idea of where their current level of evolution stands, for it helps us identify what challenges and influences we are engaged in. If we know how and why our lives are being affected, then we may find it easier to venture inwards with correct discernment. It also helps to know what others have experienced in their respective journeys, for it can shed light on the issues we are currently facing; why sometimes we might experience powerful life upheavals and ultimately how to catalyse the unfolding transitions. In so doing, we can remove much unnecessary doubt, fear, pain and anguish. It is for these key reasons I offer my interpretation in this book.

I do not offer my views as 'The Absolute Truth', for it is my belief that each of us is influenced to a greater or lesser degree by inner distortions of reality. Rather, I offer them as an interpretation of my truth, which may resonate with you at least in part and thereby help you unfold a deeper understanding of your own truth.

So how might you use this book and the guidance contained within it? My purpose has been to provide a text book offering a 'route map' through the key transitions of our lives. It is something you can continually refer to on your journey of unfolding. It excludes no particular religion, belief system or spiritual practice, providing they are allied to the universal driving force of unconditional love and operating as I believe they were always meant to - as doorways into our own direct experience. My descriptions should not be considered as dogmatic gospel. They are personal viewpoints which I trust are good enough to raise awareness as we encounter similar experiences and wonder why life is taking the twists and turns it is. Each of us is unique, walking a unique pathway and yet those who have walked before us have left signposts - milestones - which many seem to encounter and describe in similar ways. I trust therefore, that for those who are meant to hear this message, it will prove of value.

I know in my heart that the Five Gateways provide the blueprint for our Ascension. In my truth, the process is a profound gift from Benevolent Consciousness and is designed to become a global standard to serve humanity in these times of great change. It is a story that has been many thousands of years in the writing and is already perhaps the most celebrated in human history. Up to this point however, it has been concealed behind veils of misunderstanding, manipulation and disinformation. Now the time has come for humanity to dust off the pages, to read the story with fresh eyes and open hearts. It is time to stand up and reclaim our divine birthright, the gift that has been denied us for so long. The time is now. There is no other time!

The Five Gateways
-overview-

The Five Gateways on the road to full Enlightenment and Ascension are expansions through internal layers of consciousness. They tend to be accompanied by a dramatic change in our perception of reality which can be mirrored by an equally dramatic life changing circumstance - a synchronistic unplanned and unforeseen "ceremony" to mark the event. For example, it could be the ending of a relationship which although may have been difficult, brought with it a new sense of liberation; or it may be the end of a career which no longer serves; or perhaps a change in geographical location to a more uplifting environment.

These occasions bring us to a Gateway between the old consciousness and the new. We are invited to seize the day, release the outdated patterns of behaviour, step through the Gateway and unveil a more authentic way of being. The Five Gateways can be summarised as follows...

Gateway 1: "Awakening" - we awaken to the magic of the soul and our interconnectedness with all life.

Gateway 2: "Realignment" - we attune to the soul and completely surrender to its supreme governance in our lives.

Gateway 3: "Transfiguration" - a dramatic shift of perception from identification with the personality to being the Seer expressed as the soul through the bodymind.

Gateway 4: "Enlightenment" - any 'fragments' of the soul still identifying with the personality are released and 'reconnected'. The soul becomes fully integral within our being.

Gateway 5: "Resurrection" - our seven bodily vehicles of expression are finally cleansed, reactivated and re-energised. The soul unfolds into multidimensional living.

Each expansion unfolds over a period of time, which although can last many years, is currently being accelerated in this critical period of human evolution. A 'quickening' is happening all around us where Benevolent Consciousness is affording us an opportunity to step onto the 'fast track' of guided, spiritual Enlightenment. In short, we are being offered a rapid reacquaintance with our divine birthright.

If we start to watch ourselves in and through all our interactions in life, then we will begin to notice every moment seems to have a natural energetic flow directing us. If we stay attentive, we are caused to see how inner tightness, generated by our conditioned programming, disrupts this flow by projecting disharmony into our outer lives. It may seem like we have reached a crossroads where it can be quite difficult to rationalise the best way forwards. Our fear of the unknown may cloud our discernment and dim our senses.

At such crossroads, the universe is inviting us to confront and let go of these inner constraints, limitations and expectations that bind us and instead express our highest truth. If we can summon the courage to follow the guiding flow of the universe, events will be carefully crafted to maintain focussed attention on our limiting patterns of behaviour. As we are caused to expose and then release our attachments to the external drama, the inner constriction is eased and our consciousness is now able to expand through that particular Gateway. We release that which was previously limiting the radiance of our soul.

The Gateway transitions themselves should not be considered as a simple doorways, but perhaps better as specific 'corridors of expansion' each with an entrance and exit. They can be transitioned relatively quickly or take many years to complete; it all depends on our recognition of what is going on for us and our degree of surrender to the process. The more we fight or deny the truth, the more prolonged the transition becomes. However, the expansions cannot be planned or manipulated; although we can accelerate them, we cannot short cut them. Unless we have consciously integrated what we are meant to, we cannot truly transition the Gateway. This does not mean that we must have an intellectual understanding of the transitions for them to take place; however, there will be a marked inner knowing that something has changed within us. In other words, we will feel the shift of consciousness.

The key is to always be in observation of our inner motivations and responses to external events, until we understand why and how our beingness is shaping the events in the first place. Each consequence, that our attention is specifically drawn to, is an outward reflection of our internal configuration of consciousness. As we step into the corridor of expansion, it seems that the key aspects for us to realise are happening with increasing regularity and we feel a strong inner compulsion to engage in the synchronistic patterning of events.

How do we know if we are making a Gateway transition?
If we surrender to the play, we will soon recognise that we have entered a specific period addressing repetitive cycles of actions and reactions. Synchronicity is the underlying code and when we begin to read it, we are caused to see where we are acting out conditioned and distorted behaviour programs arising from fixed neural pathways in the brain. These are formed from the perceived need for a particular outcome in life.

These pathways prevent spontaneous authentic action by the soul; the soul is veiled by them and is unable to radiate its true essence. As we bring conscious awareness to the distortions, we notice that they generate tightness throughout the bodymind, as we are sucked into de-energising programmed loops of activity.

However, if we can resist responding to this tightness by realising and releasing our attachment, then we become able to switch identification from the tightness of the bodymind and instead to the lightness and expansiveness of the soul. A new way of expressing is revealed to us - a gift of beingness - which helps us bypass the old behaviour. If we keep attuning to this lightness, then the old constriction dissolves, our consciousness expands and eventually our vibration rises to the level required to pass through the Gateway.

How do we know if we have passed through a Gateway?
As previously mentioned, each passing is marked by a ceremony of one form or another (previously known as an "initiation"). The ceremony can be very dramatic and alter the outward experiences of one's life permanently. It could shatter and break apart some or all of our existing relationships; it may feel as if we are going through a crisis or some kind of breakdown (sometimes called "spiritual emergence") or it may feel as if life is bringing us to the very threshold of endurance. It is as if we have studied a new facet of beingness and are now being examined to see if we have gained the necessary experience to sustain that new way of being.

However, we should not consider we are being judged in some way, for the expansion is self determining. Although the event might be testing and painful, if we can summon the courage to confront our fears, we will pass through the Gateway, whereupon the sense of release, expansion and liberation can be truly breathtaking and divinely magical. So when we feel the fear arising, if instead of turning sheepishly away, we can look it square in the eyes and walk courageously into the jaws of uncertainty, then the bubble of illusion will miraculously explode and we will emerge bathed in a new radiant light.

Although often quite dramatic, it is also possible that we have transitioned one or more of the Gateways in previous lifetimes, in which case, we may recreate much milder repetitions in the current lifetime to remind us. Neither should we consider that having transitioned a Gateway, our consciousness is then somehow fixed in the new expansion. It is also possible to slip backwards if we do not remain self vigilant. The journey forwards requires continual commitment, perseverance and attention to our inner state of being.

It is also important to say, that although the Gateways are described as a step by step progression, they are not simply linear. It could be, for example, that even though our consciousness is centred in Gateway 1, we may also begin to process karma which would not normally be fully engaged until Gateway 4. Likewise, although we may begin to experience multidimensionality quite early in our journey, this would normally be associated with opening Gateway 5. Indeed, perhaps for this reason, I have observed a definite tendency for most people to overestimate where they are in the process. True and lasting progression depends on non-attachment, especially to the need for progress!

To me, the Gateways could perhaps best be considered as a multi-dimensional spiral staircase, with each higher Gateway enfolding the earlier ones. It is therefore of value to read and digest all of the Gateways information, even though we might be at an earlier stage in our journey. If we observe with complete self honesty and watch where the ego might want to raise its head, then we may truly perceive where we are on our path, thereby gaining deep understanding of how and why our lives are being influenced as they are. It can smooth our evolution and prevent any unnecessary meanderings down blind alley ways!

In the following five sections, we will look at these divine expansions in detail, including tools, tips and advice for transitioning the Five Gateways shared from real life experiences.

Gateway 1
"Awakening"

*"Know that this universe is nothing but a dream,
a bluff of nature
to test your consciousness of immortality."*

Paramahansa Yogananda

Key: Surrender

From the author's memoirs...

My life was changed forever on 29th November 2002 by an event that would be etched in my consciousness for all eternity. A benevolent presence was with me as I sat behind the steering wheel of a smashed car obstructing the fast lane of the M40 just north of Oxford. It was a typically busy day with cars travelling at their usual breakneck speed. I looked up through the driver's side window to see the yellow driving lights of a fast approaching car only yards away. In the next moment, a mere blink of the eye, it would career headlong into mine and I would be dead. Yet I did not mind, it felt like this was meant to happen. A part of me was already in heaven, the rest was about to join it.

Why was I so at peace? Why was I positively looking forward to my own death? Up to that point, I had been living a lie; a forty year old business man with wife and two children leading a rapidly expanding web development company, an executive lifestyle with an executive car and house to match. I had all the trappings of a successful consumeristic life style, everything we in society are conditioned to aspire to. Yet nothing seemed to satisfy me. There was always the search for something else as yet unknown. Earlier, I had managed to momentarily pacify my discontent with better cars, gadgets, clothes or music. When these failed, adrenaline sports took over and most Sundays you'd find me careering down a rocky mountain pass on my top-of-the-range mountain bike or deeply engaged in my other form of reality avoidance - the martial arts.

In truth I was clinically depressed. My thirteen year marriage had been on the rocks for some years. Unlike the tired Friday night videos, we were not "living life happily ever after". We had long since lost genuine interest in each other and the vacuum of true soul connection had been filled by predictable mutual dependency. My life was determined by pleasing others because, in truth, I lacked the courage to be genuine and speak my honest feelings: pleasing my children on a Saturday at Whacky Warehouse because I had lost the ability to do something original; pleasing my friends by fulfilling their conditioned expectations of me; pleasing ridiculously demanding customers because I needed that ever burgeoning pay cheque. I was truly lost in the rat race, climbing the endless property ladder to nowhere. Something just had to give... and finally, just when all hope seemed to be lost, life did give. It gave more than I could ever - in my wildest dreams - imagine possible.

It had begun a few weeks earlier with an email, "the chance of a lifetime", an all expenses paid trip to Comdex, the international technology conference in Las Vegas. There was just one more vacant place available to the first applicant. The thought of winning never entered my mind, but something deep within caused me to apply anyway. Surprise, surprise! I won the last place and a few weeks later, just like Alice, I was whisked off to a magical wonderland. As the plane steadily emerged out of the dark, billowing clouds shrouding Heathrow International Airport, there was a deepening sense that I was leaving the darkness and density of my past behind. Midflight entertainment was the film "The Bourne Identity", the story of a betrayed man, shot several times in the back and cast adrift in the ocean. Miraculously discovered by the crew of a fishing trawler, he is rescued and healed, but left suffering amnesia, unaware of his true identity. Comfortably numb I may have been, but even so, I could not miss the startling synchronistic parallel with my own life. Indeed, from the very beginning, there was a sense of magic in the air, a presence, seemingly able to shape events like my encounter with Maria, a wonderfully warm and sharing soul who helped me to let go - just for a moment - of the depression and hopelessness of my meaningless life, which now seemed many worlds away.

One of the Seven Wonders of the World, the Grand Canyon, is but a short flight from Las Vegas and in my current mood of surrender, a trip there with Maria seemed infinitely more appealing than back-to-back seminars courtesy of corporate America. As we stared together into the majestic void, the feeling that we were stood on the very precipice of life itself, gripped the core of my being. Perhaps it was this infinite stillness that sparked off the inner alchemy to finally abandon the annoying chatter of my childlike ego. Perhaps it was the growing feeling of a guiding presence or the deep yearning of my long abandoned soul cast adrift in the ocean of life. Whatever it was, something had called me from my bed early the following morning to the roof top of the Hilton hotel where we were staying.

Martial Arts was a passion of mine, it had always seemed to keep my head above the engulfing tide of mass human subconsciousness. So it was, I found myself practising gently flowing movements in the early morning darkness high above the crisscrossing matrix of city streets far below me. But this was quite unlike any other practice I had ever experienced. What began quite casually became increasingly sublime; somehow each move was drawing me deeper inside myself. Suddenly, I became both the movement and the moved dissolving into a new effortlessness, where flow happened spontaneously. There was no longer anyone inside saying "go" or "stop", "turn" or "block". Crystal clear clarity was arising from within as the inner and outer worlds unfolded into one. Then on the horizon, attention (at this point I cannot even say 'my' attention) was drawn to the sky beginning to lighten, the blackness becoming purple and indigo as dawn gently kissed the distant panorama. At the sun's first appearance, I was compelled to stop. Frozen in time, I noticed the early morning chatter of traffic far below me receding further and further into seemingly distant galaxies until there was no sound at all. Nothing was worthy of this stillness, of this beauty, of this peace.

Time ground to a halt and yet simultaneously accelerated. Within the apparent blink of an eye, the sun was fully up and radiating golden warmth. Suddenly I was being washed through with wave upon wave of unconditional love, seemingly from a source of infinite benevolence. Release after release, unfolding upon unfolding, surrender upon surrender. I was being loved completely and wholly just for me. There was no judgment in the love and no need for anything to be reciprocated. It seemed to penetrate every fibre of my being, seeing me with complete openness, honesty and clarity. It saw my darkness and loved me not in spite of it like another human might: no, it loved me BECAUSE of it. For the first time in all the forty years of my life, I was totally accepted and worthy. Being 'me' in that moment was entirely and completely right. No one was criticising, questioning, abusing or insinuating. There was not even the requirement for a payback, no need for me to reciprocate. I was allowed to swim in it, to sink in it, to breathe it into every pore. This was my initiation to the magical, universal flow of divine love I have come to know as the "Awakening" - this was the reason I had no fear of death that day.

Ten days later, as I sat in the crumpled wreckage awaiting the inevitable smash of a fast approaching car, the guiding presence was with me. Time had ground to a halt, my consciousness expanded and suddenly I was coexisting in two places at once. In the higher one, I could feel the lightness, expansion and infinite peace indicating at-one-ment with the whole of creation. In the lower, I was watching a movie, the story of my life thus far. I was caused to see how every event in our lives has but one purpose; to help us reveal an aspect of truth about ourselves to ourselves. A magical orchestra of synchronicity shapes and forms ceaseless patterns of activity with just one intent; to wake us up to the glorious magic of everlasting divine union.

Each moment of my life's review invited me to see that we shape every experience according to our inner tightness. Whatever we fear, whatever we are attached to, whatever sense of lack we may have, we recreate in our lives time and again until eventually we get the message; that we are already whole and complete; that we do not need anything but that inner sense of contentment; that we do not need to effort or struggle in our lives; we do not need to shape, control or manifest. Simply by letting go, our inner constriction unwinds and the negative patterns of our lives can dissolve. In so doing, our vibrational energy rises and our consciousness expands to fill the universe. This is why I was fully prepared to die, because I knew I couldn't die! Death was merely a doorway into another more expanded state of being.

During the final moments of my life's review, I was treated to a spectacular vision. An event of such cosmic proportions that it is impossible to properly justify in words. I saw two overlapping worlds separating through a brilliant galactic sunrise - a stunning supernova - which seemed to fill the night sky to eternity. The light body of our planetary system was ascending into a higher, more evolved state of being. She was positively pulsating with universal life energy. The old world, on the other hand, was becoming darker and denser. As Gaia expanded into her glorious new form, her old body was crumbling away like a tired, old skin; she was shaking off that consciousness still lost in the control, manipulation, doubt, fear and denial. I was ready to join the new dawning. In that moment, I was able to let go of everything and surrender to the inevitable. As I awaited the smash of the fast approaching car, I was in an ecstatic state of profound bliss.

What happened next was beyond the realm of my 'normal' comprehension. No, I did not ascend into some heavenly nirvana and neither did the fast approaching car career headlong into mine. Instead, the car door opened and an 'angelic' individual helped me out of the crumpled wreckage. As I was guided back across the motorway to the hard shoulder, I looked to my left to see that every car on the busy midday motorway had miraculously stopped, forming a perfect parting line along which I was now walking. Mine was the only car involved in an incident which, under normal circumstances, would have resulted in a multi car pileup.

Neither I nor anyone else was meant to die that day. The presence made me aware that it was my purpose to continue, to share a message with those prepared to listen. "Five Gateways" is that message and I had just passed through Gateway 1.

Gateway 1
-overview-

For many lifetimes, we have lived completely unaware of the presence of the soul and our magical oneness with all life. This process of forgetting our inherent nature in order to remember it again, has been pre-planned and necessary, for we cannot know what we truly are, unless we have first known what we are not. Just as we cannot know hot without knowing cold, we cannot partake of the infinite, unbounded liberation unless we have first been confined and constricted.

This constriction has been delivered by an illusion which we created for ourselves. As "The One Life", at the Big Bang, we divided into multiplicity of form and universal awareness arose from the interplay between the separate parts. These parts flowed outwards to ever increasing separation, what we might call "Separation Consciousness". However, since everything came from nothing, the outward flow must be balanced by an equal and opposite inward one, which we may call "Unity Consciousness". Although nothing is separate, we were able to create the notion of relativity (and therefore individual form) from the two opposing flows of energy. After eons of time, even before time itself, Unity Consciousness evolved into individual souls providing the possibility of unique and varied experience. Our journey has been one of false identification. By design, we have lost ourselves within the notion of separation and tied ourselves into the external drama, believing that the answer to our questions, needs, fears, hopes and desires can somehow be found by shaping (or at least trying to shape) Separation Consciousness...

"A human being is a part of the whole called by us
universe, a part limited in time and space.
He experiences himself, his thoughts and feelings
as something separated from the rest,
a kind of optical delusion of his consciousness.
This delusion is a kind of prison for us,
restricting us to our personal desires
and to affection for a few persons nearest to us.
Our task must be to free ourselves from this prison
by widening our circle of compassion
to embrace all living creatures
and the whole of nature in its beauty."
Albert Einstein

Eventually we begin to surrender and give up chasing soullessly through the external world of consequences. We tire of continually trying to shape, control and manipulate because even if we manage a tenuous degree of security, absolute control is always frustratingly just beyond our grasp. There will always be something to rock the foundations of our precious existence no matter how financially secure or sensually satisfied we might think we are. Eventually, we abandon the fruitless torture of trying to please others, realising that it is only they who can find their own pleasure as a result of their internal state of being. It is at this point, the inner world of causality beckons - that which governs the outer circumstances of our lives.

As we begin to relinquish the struggle, the Gordian knot of attachment begins to unwind of its own accord. Sometimes this can be sudden and dramatic as in a life threatening car crash for example. Or, it could be the stunning recognition of the awesome majesty of Mother Nature; sitting down on a park bench, quietly watching the sun streaming through gently waving branches or looking out into the star filled night sky, touching the vastness of space, finally realising the shocking inconsequence of our "storm-in-a-tea-cup" lives.

It is just as we surrender the need to shape, manipulate and control, that the first key to the true nature of our authentic reality materialises. Frequently, the door of our prison cell is unlocked as the result of a curious or even dramatic occurrence. It could be an event that causes us to question the very fabric of reality or an unusual phenomenon that seems to connect us to life in a way we have not tasted before. Maybe for an instant, we feel our interconnectedness; we do not just see an animal through the clouded haze of a tired memory, but feel its very life essence coursing through our veins. It might be staring at the clouds and dissolving into them; it could be the experience of timelessness; the sense of spiritual presence or waves of unconditional love irradiating our being. Suddenly, we are no longer in a prison cell, it is inside of us.

All such experiences indicate that our consciousness has expanded - just a little bit - out of the tea cup and into the universe. We taste the magic of the soul for the first time. When this happens, it tends to be that we then embark on another journey in search of more of that taste and paradoxically, the quest often ratchets up the internal efforting once more, so we may slip frustratingly back into our previous slumber. Unlike before however, we now have a memory of the soul, so although we are not directly experiencing the expanded consciousness of the Awakening itself, it could be that we think we are. This period in our unfolding is called by some the "pre-Awakening"; we are being the seeker, but never quite finding. The mind is chasing old memories.

The pre-Awakening can last many years until we tire yet again, give up the quest for the Holy Grail and settle once more into the awesomely ordinary and profound simplicity of our own self awareness. It is then, in our surrendered solitude, that the constriction of life's unfulfilled promises can finally burst wide open. That which we have always sought was always present. We did not have to pilgrimage, seek or search, the pot of gold at the end of our life's rainbow was all the time, right under our very feet!

When this new dawn arises, no matter what then transpires, whatever tightness we may once more project ourselves into, there is always a way back to this experience. We may frequently submerge ourselves back into the depths of delusion, but somehow, eventually we keep remembering to let go and then bob back up again to the surface, gasping for a few welcome breaths of crystal clear air.

It is when we are able to continually do this, that we can say we are truly "Awakened". The experience of the soul has been initiated within our being and we sense its presence on a frequent basis. We have expanded through Gateway 1 to the magical taste of Unity Consciousness, that awesome awareness which unites all.

Transitioning Gateway 1
-useful tools-

1. Be ready to let go: *be absolutely clear that we are ready to relinquish the struggle to shape external circumstances - the drama.*
2. Be the Observer: *move to the place of the Observer of ourselves as much as possible.*
3. Regaining the Observer: *develop a technique for continually returning to the place of the Observer.*
4. Surrender into complete self acceptance: *let go of self judgment and surrender into complete self acceptance.*
5. Mark the Awakening: *notice the internal shift of consciousness that is the Awakening and watch for a memorable ceremony marking the event.*

1. Be ready to let go: *be absolutely clear that we are ready to relinquish the struggle to shape external circumstances - the drama.* It seems like an obvious point, but although many people say they realise that absolute truth lies beyond their day-to-day activities in the illusion and, even though they say they have tired of seeking external gratification to fulfil a need of inner completeness, they are not ready to change. Their conditioning and strength of addiction to conditioned behaviours is too strong for them to overcome at the moment. For example, the fear of giving up a job that is crushing the soul; reluctance to end an unfulfilling and restrictive relationship; the fear of spending time alone in stillness; fear of change and what that might bring. It may be that we are simply not ready to let go of such constriction. In which case, probably the best approach is to keep doing these things, until finally there is complete acceptance, that the path of self realisation will provide the only route to liberation. So we continue to give in to the conditioned behaviours until we realise that they can never bring the fulfilment and sense of completeness we are really looking for. When we have finally tired and sickened of the struggle and internal efforting caused by our need to shape the circumstances of our lives - the drama - then we are ready to embark on the inner journey of self discovery.

At this point, be absolutely clear that the ONLY game going on in the universe is self realisation and that we might as well finally take an active part in that game, rather than trying to conveniently ignore it while it plays with us! So accept that ALL events, happenings and circumstances have but one purpose... to discover our absolute completeness - our "absoluteness" - beyond all circumstances. Realise the aim of the game is to be completely free inside WHATEVER happens.

2. Be the Observer: *move to the place of the Observer of ourselves as much as possible.*
When we have finally made the choice to venture inwards, the next step is to begin watching ourselves in all activities, events and circumstances. In other words, we become the Observer of ourselves. We may define the Observer as a personality led intention to act; it is an aspect of mind. We notice where we lose our temper;

where we become tight inside because of other people's behaviour; where our addictions to something in particular cause us to act in predictable ways. For example, we are not able to follow a spontaneous pull from the soul because we are hungry and need to eat, or we are not able to sit in stillness because we are attached to distraction, or when our behaviour is dictated by the perceived need to please or placate someone else. When we notice this, firstly it is important just to watch it, accept it as a conditioned behaviour which although is our responsibility to deal with, is not our fault for it being there in the first place; it likely came from the circumstances of our upbringing and the society we live in.

In this way, we do not judge ourselves for giving in to the behaviours and therefore begin to liberate ourselves from the identity that has formed around them. At this point, it is vitally important that we do not try to cure the attachments by using techniques such as Hypnotherapy or Neuro-Linguistic Programming, for all we end up doing is cementing ourselves as an identity, albeit a different one. For example, "I am the identity that has covered up my lack of inner completeness by forcing myself to give up smoking or binge eating". Or, "I am the identity that has cloaked my lack of self esteem by continually reminding myself to be confident", or "I am the identity that has to control my body language in order to appear confident". When we are able to watch ourselves in these dramas and not need to change them, we are actually already freeing ourselves from them.

When we are being the Observer of all arising experience, this is really what it means to be meditating. Whilst some may like to engage in a particular meditative practice such as chanting, breathing or sitting in stillness, others find it just as effective to be engaged in everyday activities. The key question is, are we lost in activity or observing ourselves in it? To me, the latter is meditating. In this state, ultimately the Observer itself will dissolve into the experience of non-identified presence - the Seer - which is to be in an enlightened state; in which case, life itself becomes meditation.

3. Regaining the Observer: *develop a technique for continually returning to the place of the Observer.*
In the beginning, we all lose the place of the Observer to a greater or lesser degree. It could be that we spend complete days lost in the "Matrix" of conditioned behaviours and controlling thought forms. At some point however, the realisation will dawn once more that we have become identified again and need to recover our centre. It could be for example that we have gone through a very difficult experience which has pushed all our inner buttons; maybe we have endured a particularly stressful time at work or difficulty in family relationships.

To help release ourselves from the drama again and recover the place of the unattached Observer, it helps to have a tool or technique to recover that place. It could be a visualisation, deep breathing or a mantra of some kind. It could be simply catching ourselves, taking a brief pause and connecting once more with the fullness of the moment. It could be something very basic, my partner for example placed post-it notes saying "let go" all around her flat. For her, something so simple was yet extremely effective!

In the work that I currently do helping people awaken, I've advocated frequently asking one's self the following questions. I have found they can be of great help...

(i) Who am I? Answer: "I am"
We are everything and nothing - the absolute beyond all definition. We are eternal, we cannot die and we cannot go anywhere because we exist everywhere. We created everything we are now experiencing and there is nothing we cannot cope with.
(ii) Why am I here? Answer: "to remember who I am"
There is only one true purpose of the universe - to experience ourselves as the Absolute - whole and complete without need of anything. Every moment reveals this to us and there is absolutely nothing else going on other than this.

(iii) What time is it? Answer: "the time is now"

Nothing before this moment matters because we can do nothing to change it and the future unfolds out of what we do in the present so we need not dwell in that either. Therefore the only thing to do is be fully present in the moment of now.

(iv) What do I need? Answer: "nothing I don't already have"

We do not need anything but ourselves to be whole and complete in this moment, because if we did, we would not be here! We will always have EXACTLY what we need to be the True Self. It is only when we are being the false self (in other words when we are identifying with the personality) that we experience lack, loss, need or desire.

4. Surrender into complete self acceptance: *let go of self judgment and surrender into complete self acceptance*

We are conditioned from birth that a sense of completeness and wholeness comes from an external 'fix'. For most of us, the love we felt in the womb comes with conditions in the external world. So we are rewarded if we are being 'good', chastised if we are being 'naughty'. We learn how certain behaviours bring fulfilment and others bring pain. As we grow, society teaches us that we are somehow not quite good enough as we are, that there is something we need externally to fulfil ourselves. These patterns of behaviour develop into a neural web program called the "inner child". We then tend to respond to all external occurrences through this identity filter. It negatively effects every decision we make, locking us into a limited and restricted reality.

As we transition puberty, powerful flows of hormones through the body cause us to rebel against this victimisation. We master new techniques and new behaviours for protecting the inner child and a new web of fixed neural pathways form in the brain acting as a second filter - the "inner teenager". Indeed, it is possible for multiple personalities to develop, especially when we have had an extremely influential experience or lasting trauma. All of these personalities can influence our every choice in life if we allow them to.

The key to releasing ourselves is to begin to notice when they are active by watching when we become tight or stressed out. It tends to happen when we feel we are being judged by another or by society in general; for example that there is something wrong with what we feel is inherently right. In truth, we are judging ourselves because we have believed we are not good enough. We can release ourselves from these programs by realising that whilst it is our responsibility to deal with this condition, it is most definitely not our fault. It is certain that it came from our upbringing and society in general.

It is vital not to descend into blame - those who influenced us were themselves conditioned by society. This opens the path to forgiveness both for them and ourselves. When we can accept neither they nor we are to blame, then we can finally accept our 'faults' not needing to change them (at least for the moment) and eventually settle into absolute self acceptance.

So the key is SURRENDER. Surrender the need for an outcome and the need to defend ourselves in any situation; be awesomely okay with whatever happens knowing that it is what we are being on the inside which really counts. Surrendering in this way, at whatever apparent personal cost, is a powerful catalyst for the Awakening.

5. Mark the Awakening: *notice the internal shift of consciousness that is the Awakening and watch for a memorable ceremony marking the event.*
When we finally release ourselves from attachment to the external drama, it comes with a quite dramatic shift of consciousness - what begins in the mind, is experienced throughout the body. So, for example, we may feel a growing sense of release, expansion, timelessness or opening up. We may experience surges of energy or waves of unconditional love flowing through us. These are all signs

that the Awakening has taken place. In which case, we may fully accept and embrace the new consciousness as our new state of being by completely immersing ourselves in it. Watch for a quite major event (a divorce for example) inviting us to mark the occasion and take full part in it with total commitment and energy. Thus our Awakening ceremony takes place.

Transitioning Gateway 1
-general misconceptions-

1. Striving: when we hear about the path to Spiritual Enlightenment and get an initial taste of it during the pre-Awakening, there frequently arises an inner striving for success. This simply pushes the 'objective' further away, in the same way a small child might try to grasp and chase a balloon. However, if we can simply rest in awareness, the 'objective' instead moves to us. In other words we realise it was there all along.

2. Not seeing the Observer: it is often erroneously imagined that when we connect with our inner Observer, we will see or feel something different and if we do not feel that, there is a tendency to assume we are not connected with it. The Observer is a state of awareness. It cannot be seen, touched, heard or felt. We are in the place of the Observer when we are continually processing what is happening in our thoughts, feelings and immediate environment.

3. Curing the tightness: when we become the Observer and feel tightness, efforting, injury, illness or disease in the bodymind, there is often the misconceived desire to want to heal it - to take the pain away. The genuine purpose of the disorder is to act as a mirror to realise that we are infinite freedom totally unidentified with such things. Trying to heal the pain simply gives it more energy and sucks us into it. To truly awaken, is to become awesomely okay with whatever is arising in the bodymind. Paradoxically, it is only when we are free of the need to be healed that true healing can take place.

4. Discipline: we are truly blessed by the abundance of many excellent spiritual practices helping people to awaken. However, all too often, we hear erroneously (in my view) that only a disciplined approach such as a particular meditation done at particular times throughout the day is the way forwards. Whilst discipline can be of value, it can also become a doctrine, which in turn removes us from the spontaneous authenticity of the soul, expressed uniquely in the moment. If we keep attuning to the soul - in other words to what brings us joy and fulfilment - then we are likely to find discipline being replaced by a continually evolving natural rhythm.

5. We must get rid of the ego: it seems to be a commonly held misconception that we must 'get rid of the ego' (the personality) in order to awaken to the oneness existing through all things. The One Life that we are, is expressed through a gloriously colourful, multi faceted, abundance of form. Take a look around at the natural world; is not each species of plant and animal displaying a widely varied characteristic of that One Life? So it is with us. Our personalities are uniquely crafted and gifted to express the many varied faces of the one Seer. It is not our ego we must get rid of, rather our attachment to it. It is only ego that tries to get rid of ego.

Transitioning Gateway 1
-signs of beginning-

Typically the Awakening is a kind of bittersweet experience. As we grow increasingly dissatisfied with society, feelings of frustration, anger or depression may arise as we begin to notice the seeming pointlessness of the external drama in which we are engaged.

As we give up trying to shape the drama, frustration may give way to listlessness and we may become increasingly distracted in day-to-day activities. We may notice that we are becoming increasingly at odds with the people around us, especially if they are still deeply engaged in the drama. It becomes ever more difficult to summon the energy to remain in these places of lower vibration.

This may cause us to break down in tears quite frequently. If this happens, the key is to allow the tears to flow for they will release pent up frustration, negative energy and disharmony. They will help wash and cleanse the convoluted energy that has built up within. These feelings may be accompanied by an inner yearning to 'go home' without fully understanding what this really means; that we are now reconnecting with Unity Consciousness, our at-one-ment with the whole of life.

Although this yearning to go home could, in extreme cases, lead even to suicidal tendencies, it is quite natural because we have recognised there is a place much more appropriate for us to be. It is just that we have forgotten that its beauty lies all around us and we have disconnected from that. It is this reconnection that feels like coming home. It is then that a state of hyperawareness may spontaneously arise precipitating the reconnection to the soul.

As this commences, we may begin to have unusual dreams, both sleeping and waking, challenging the very essence of what we have come to know as reality. Often these dreams are of a prophetic nature, guiding us on the journey of Awakening. In summary, typical signs that the Awakening may be commencing are as follows...

- a growing realisation that nothing in the external world seems to fully satisfy;
- frustration or underlying depression at the state of one's life;
- an arising feeling of disconnection from society;
- feelings of listlessness and lack of direction;
- prophetic, reoccurring dreams questioning the nature of reality;
- feelings of hyperawareness;
- noticing strange coincidences;
- a sense of 'magic' in the air.

Transitioning Gateway 1
-signs of completion-

Someone who has passed through Gateway 1 will be feeling the soul and its magical presence in their lives. They will be tasting the wonder of at-one-ment with all things. The intensity of experience through the five senses will have made a dramatic leap, as though the 'volume' was suddenly increased. No longer are we viewing life through the tired mental filters of memories and ideas, rather we are feeling our magical connection with its essence. For example, in seeing a horse, we can no longer simply pass it by as an ordinary, everyday experience. Instead, we might be brought to tears by the sheer magnificence of it.

Those involved in the moving arts such as dancing, gymnastics, athletics, yoga or tai chi are no longer simply performing a repetitive practice, rather they are tuning deeply into bodily awareness allowing it to speak for them. Such depth and intensity of experience can frequently bring one to tears. The same may be said for music, painting, writing and singing. All are now opening channels directly to the soul.

Conversely, it becomes increasingly difficult to witness the suffering of another, be they human, plant or animal and we begin to feel their suffering as our own. Whilst we may realise that all experiences are designed to bring self realisation, it does not prevent deep empathy and compassion arising within. Sometimes these feelings may be lost within the daily routine of life, but someone who has successfully made this first transition will have discovered ways of reconnecting, whether it be a few moments breathing, a favourite meditation, or a walk in the countryside for example.

In summary, this reconnection to the soul may be typically experienced as follows...

- *feelings of awesome okayness, sense of lightness or floatiness;*
- *dissolving of the sense of want, ambition and need;*
- *sense of expansiveness and timelessness;*
- *feelings of interconnectedness and at-one-ment with all things;*
- *increased intensity of experiences through the five senses;*
- *observation of magical and/or 'miraculous' events;*
- *initial unveiling of psychic sensitivity and intuition;*
- *tingling sensations or pulsations in the hands;*
- *feelings of joy and waves of love passing through the body.*

Gateway 1
-summary-

The Awakening is one of the most profoundly beautiful experiences the miracle of creation has blessed us with. Prior to it, in most cases we will have blindly accepted our separateness from all things. Whilst we may have held the notion of a creator - God - we have experienced ourselves as separate from that Source of All Life, not the integral whole we all are.

We endure countless lifetimes in this delusion, totally engrossed in the alluring seduction of the external drama, until finally one day, we awaken to the first realisation: that nothing 'out there' ever seems to fully satisfy; we are always left wanting more of one experience or less of another. We know there is something we are ultimately looking for, but we are not entirely sure what it is or how to find it. Perhaps a new job, a new living environment or that perfect partner that never seems to quite materialise?

With the realisation that the solution to our problem is continually alluding us, finally we may give up the chase and paradoxically, just when we stop trying to grasp at the balloon dancing continuously just out of reach, suddenly the illusion bursts. An awesomely simple inner knowing arises over us: that we are everything; that we need nothing; that we are - and always have been - already complete. The love and fulfilment we have ceaselessly chased was there inside us all along and we do not need any one else to give it to us. Finally, laughingly, we sob outrageously at our foolishness, until we settle into the stillness of shockingly simple self acceptance...

"There is one great cosmic joke
that we have been continually having
at our own expense throughout all eternity.
It is the delusion that we may find happiness,
contentment, fulfilment or love as a direct
result of something at large in
the external universe of effects.
Finally, one magical day, the absolute
truth of causality beckons, that we are
- and always have been -
the creators and therefore masters of our own experience.
At which point, we either laugh or sob outrageously
both at the incredulity of our ignorance
and the awesome majesty of our Being"
Openhand

As we give up the struggle, we surrender internally, thereby releasing inner constriction and tightness. Our consciousness expands and we reconnect with our soul which has until now faithfully lingered, concealed in the background shadows of our day-to-day experience. At which point, we are awakened to the conscious life force existing in all things. Our divine connection to the nurturing soul of Mother Earth becomes undeniably apparent.

As we taste the beauty and magic of oneness with all things, it is likely that we will experience both joy and sorrow; the joy of rediscovering a long lost friend and the sorrow at the recognition of what our collective ignorance has been doing to that friend. Frequently there follows the stunning recognition that society has been as a rabid infestation, a rapidly spreading plague devouring all in its path, destroying both plant, animal and human alike.

We realise that all the while, the guiding hand of Benevolent Consciousness has been speaking to us through the harmonistic orchestra of synchronicity. We see how the Matrix of mass human subconsciousness has been continually at odds with this natural weave from which the fabric of all events is woven. It is then that we are humbled, brought to our very knees by the simplest of things, a honey bee perhaps, a flowering rose or the early morning dew dropping from an open leaf. How is it that such seemingly basic things can be completely at one when we, with all our supposed intelligence, have been so completely lost?

When we are truly Awakened, it becomes impossible to pollute, to damage, to manipulate or to kill ANY LIVING CREATURE, unless to do so is to the benefit of our whole natural ecosystem. We do not sit there trying to figure out a cure for global warming just to continue to serve our own selfish addictions or delusionary needs; the higher harmony is not about finding more efficient and sustainable ways to exploit Mother Earth. There is simply the inner compulsion to be as one with the whole of life at whatever apparent personal cost to ourselves.

Finally, we may come to the realisation that some global meltdown of society might be exactly what is necessary, to bring those who will listen, back to their senses and into alignment with the natural evolutionary path of our planet. Whatever the pain that such an event might bring, whatever the chaos, maybe it is exactly what we need to further our own evolution. After all...

"destruction is construction when it contains the seeds of the future"

If we follow the current flow of events, it is clear that many are still resistant to the changes going on all around us. The conditioning of society seems simply too strong for them to break free of their own accord. Our leaders and governments are still trying relentlessly to manipulate the external drama according to old world agendas, instead of working with people to go into the heart and reconnect with the benevolent life force through all things. Hence we are witnessing an increasing polarity between light and dark.

If the resistance continues, the tension will increase, but ultimately, nothing will be able to deny the movement into the higher truth. Anything that is of the lower harmony will crumble and fall. This is the natural order of things. It is inevitable. The movement into the higher paradigm is our destiny and any concentration of consciousness that maintains an eddy current in this eternal flow of life, will ultimately be unwound. Even the hardest granite gets washed away by the softest flow.

If current trends continue, it is likely that many who are still indoctrinated will not heed the warnings. Does this mean those who are awakening might as well continue to pollute, deforest and destroy anyway? Far from it. Our planetary system is ascending and, to join it, we must become as one with it. This means to cherish it and nurture it as our own selves. As the old world structures topple around us, indeed there will be much difficulty and even chaos, but this old world will provide the bridge - the testing ground - for the new one. We must unfold the higher harmony and live it fully, here and now, if we are to progress further forwards.

Even if you believed the physical world could come to an end tomorrow, would you still plant that apple tree today? An awakened soul probably would.

Gateway 2
"Realignment"

"Between stimulus and response there is a space...
In that space is our power to choose our response.
In our response lies our growth and our freedom."
Viktor Frankl

Key: follow your joy

From the Author's memoirs...

I had been living in a profound state of bliss for some months. As others have described before, it was as though I could continue to watch events pass me by without needing to change or shape them. I could rest happily on the park bench of life enjoying the song of the birds, the rush of the wind, the rustle of the trees; there was no need to do, or not do, any particular thing.

Then after a while, I began to feel an inner calling guiding me forwards. Not as before though, this voice was not of the mind. It sang from somewhere much deeper than that. It was the quiet melody of an ancient and yet timeless music, the vibration of a bygone era that was calling me back to my essence - the memory of the original condition of unity. It was my soul singing to me, that which arises from the Source and flows back to it. I had made the journey to the far reaches of the universe - absolute separation from God - and it was now time to make the journey home again to the living breathing experience of unity.

My soul was a mystical siren singing the sweet song of surrender... "Ride on my wave and I will take you on a magical journey of remembering who you are and where you came from, a journey of such profound ecstasy; it is a story you've been writing for many lifetimes, it is the story of you." "But how do I listen to my soul?" I asked, "How can I be guided forwards?"

No answer came. I asked again and still no answer. For a while I became frustrated and tight, slipping out of the experience of peaceful inner expansion that I had come to know. This was not right. What was the point of guidance if it took me back into the place of confinement? Then it suddenly dawned on me, the silence WAS THE ANSWER. To hear the sweet message of the soul and to have a chance of even understanding its language, I had to find silence within. I had to be free from the background noise of distorting influences. I was drawn to the coast to find stillness and for five days meditated on the cliff tops in Cornwall looking out over the natural ruggedness to the rolling ocean beyond.

Each day I sat quietly trying to still my busy mind, each time a little longer than before and yet still no message came. All the while only silence. Many times I was close to giving up. What was the point? What was I still searching for? Why not just give up and go back to the blissful state that was just awesomely okay with accepting anything and everything?

However, each time I thought to give up, something caused me to persevere, to stay just a little bit longer. I could feel the increasing tightness in my tired body; one that had been battered and bruised by the clenched fists of time; one that was toxic with the poison of modern day living; one that preferred activity to stillness. Even though I knew my body was not me, it was still there, unavoidably in the centre of my reality like a roundabout with no exits. Perhaps this was part of the message? I persevered, even if I was going in circles, at least I knew I was still not attached to the ride! As I watched these repetitive revolutions of thought, emotion and tired weariness, it suddenly dawned on me that I did not need to cure, heal or quieten them at all. Whilst I was focussing on my inner drama, I was giving it more attention, more energy, more consciousness. I was making the already noisy base drum of my inner orchestra even louder. If I wanted instead to hear the subtler, quieter instruments in the background, I simply had to notice them, to tune into them, in other words to 'attune' to them. Then in turn they would get louder and the base drum would quieten.

This changed the whole experience of my meditation. Instead I would tune into things that I noticed and then see how I felt about them inside. It might be the sound of the waves, the colour of gently undulating meadows or the movement of clouds. Suddenly I had changed the dynamic. Instead of fighting a continually losing battle, I had found a wonderful game I could always win. What had started as a rigid discipline for a given period at a set time each day, suddenly sprang into life - now my meditation was a living, breathing experience that came with me everywhere.

A feeling would come over me to stop and watch the kite surfers riding the wind and waves or a bumble bee would grab my attention as it made its busy yet effortless way from flower to flower or the gentle rustling trees on the cliff path. With no agenda, I was completely free to follow. Then, spontaneously, I would find myself just breathing, my eyes would close and I would sink deep into expansiveness. There was no intention any more, meditation - life itself - just unfolded.

It was the final day of my trip. I felt it had been successful, but somehow, there was still something missing. I hadn't yet received my message, something I could take home to remind me how to follow my soul. My vision quest had not yet been fulfilled. With this in mind, I found myself walking along the cliff path when I came across a clearing in the shrubs and brambles leading to a precipice stretching outwards like a finger pointing towards the ocean. It was the perfect spot to sit for a while and it was unmistakably beckoning me. I settled down, noticed the pull to go inwards, but not into the aching and tightness of my body, instead this time, I went into the breath. The meditation quickly intensified until breath swept me up onto its silent wings becoming first lighter and lighter, then fuller and fuller harnessing the life energy of the universe until like a wave, I swept through the pain washing over and around the rocks, now powerless to resist the inevitable flow of my soul. I quietly dissolved upon the shore of awesome okayness - the place that did not need answers.

Then a wonderful miracle of nature happened as if to reward me for my patience. As I opened my eyes a bird of prey, a kestrel, rose up the cliff and hung majestically in the air right in front of me. Shivers ran up and down my spine, an intensity of awareness connected me as one with the bird. I knew this was the message I had come for; my whole being was suddenly fixated by it. There was a deep welling up within me and tears began flowing down my cheeks. The bird connected with the very essence of my being. For a seeming eternity, it hung in the air just a few feet in front of me, skilfully angling its body and wings to harmonise with the wind, held aloft on the feather edge of effortlessness. Yet through all the fluid, free flowing movement of its body, its head was perfectly still, fixed in time and space, eyes glued intently on its target below. Suddenly, without warning, without preparation, without labour of thought or intent, the right moment had arrived; it dropped out of the sky like a bullet shooting swiftly downwards onto its prey. This was the natural order of things; wind, kestrel, prey, all as one, experiencing divine union.

I was left speechless. It took me some time to find words for the message but ultimately they came; "Be in the place of the Observer of yourself and all life without identifying with it; without judging it; without intending or needing it to be a certain way. When you are not identified in this way, your mind and heart open and you begin to feel and flow with the natural order of things. In one hand you receive the energy of the moment in truth, as it really is, without needing to change it, then with the other hand, when the moment is right, give yourself to your highest truth, that which expresses absolutely who and what you are. Everything flows as one to bring Right Action into Right Outcome".

I was blown away. Through the bird, the Soul of the Earth had spoken to me loud and clear. There was no denying, doubting or ignoring. The guiding hand of Benevolent Consciousness had granted me my message and I resolved from that moment onwards to ALWAYS listen. In the weeks that followed, I would come to realise when we make such a resolution to ourselves, we are likewise making the same affirmation to the universe and when we do so, she will gather the entire force of nature to test our resolve, to hold us to account, to see if we have the courage to really be free. She is not doing it out of spite or malice, not out of some masochistic sense of humour. We have said to her "We are free! Free to follow the divine flow of the universe, the only thing that makes sense in a tired world of humanity's broken promises". She wants that for us, it is our destiny and the only way to live it, is to test it and test it she does.

My initiation to test if I was ready to follow my soul materialised almost immediately. My marriage had been on the rocks for quite some time, but in my newly awakened state, it felt like I should make one last effort to resolve things between me and Alison "for the sake of the children" at least. Hence we embarked on a program of intensive marriage guidance counselling. We raked over the ashes, found common ground and managed to rekindle a few embers of an apparently dying fire. When all the pain, frustration and judgment had been pared away, refreshingly there remained deep feelings of mutual respect. We had shared much together over the years, joy, love, happiness and not least, two gorgeous children. Perhaps it had been the years of grafting that had taken their toll? Perhaps it was my incessant need to control our lives? Perhaps it was her laissez faire attitude to debt, punctuality and tidiness. Surely in my new state of surrender, I could be more accepting of those things and just let life be?

I was to discover surrender and acceptance are two different things. To surrender to the universe is not to blindly accept; it is to recognise the truth of what is and then follow that. The universe conjured the perfect teaching of this age old wisdom. Alison and I decided we would make a fresh start and begin it with a second honeymoon in the town of Deia on the island of Majorca. It was our favourite retreat destination and we were both keenly looking forward to it. As the plane began to trundle faster and faster towards take off, Alison turned to me, smiled and asked "Do you love me?" A sharp intake of breath overtook me and I was just about to regurgitate the classic "Of course I do my Darling" when something caught me. As before, time seemed to slow way down and an image of the hovering kestrel floated into my awareness, a superlative demonstration of absolute truth, beckoning me to do exactly the same.

I paused for what must have seemed an eternity. I knew what wanted to be said, what she wanted to hear, what my conditioned behaviours were demanding. The steamroller of controlling thought forms seemed to be gathering strength just like the now irresistibly rising aircraft. "Of course I do my Darling" was what the crowd wanted to hear, "I will love you forever". But the kestrel would not let me give in. I had to rise above mass human subconsciousness and find the truth, "I love you but... I'm not in love with you", came the words from somewhere deep within. So compelling, so filled with energy, so soulful were they, that their truth could neither be ignored nor denied, no longer swept under the carpet of tired excuses. Alison was silent, what was there to say? When you speak from the heart, everyone knows it, even those living in denial can feel it. When the soul speaks, it needs no interpretation, it can be felt by all.

In that moment, as the aircraft rose into the air flying us apparently to our bright, honeymoon destination, our marriage ended. As painful as it may have been, underneath I was singing like a bird released. This was my transition through Gateway 2. I was now following my joy, soaring on the wings of truth.

Gateway 2
-overview-

As our journey through the layers of inner consciousness accelerates, increasingly we notice the natural synchronistic order of things. Chance 'coincidences' reveal the underlying patterning of universal interconnectedness and the realisation dawns that every event has a natural flow in harmony with a greater purpose. We notice that from time to time we move into alignment with this purpose where everything feels totally magical and harmonious. It is in these moments where we feel completely 'in the groove' that we have truly attuned to our soul which is aligned with the Divine Flow.

The Gateway 2 transition, "Realignment", is about attuning to the soul until we surrender completely to its supreme governance in our lives. In other words, we have made an inner commitment that all choices in life will be those of the soul - our highest truth.

At birth, the soul infuses into the bodymind and over time begins to identify with it. Conditioned behaviours develop forming closed loops of behaviour within the brain. In our dense and often harsh environment, the light of the soul begins to dim. If our parents are not sufficiently awake to continually remind us of our divine essence, or if negative external energies are too overpowering, then the soul begins to fragment and dissipate throughout the bodymind. If this happens (as it does in most cases), we lose connection to Unity Consciousness and the chakras begin to close down, such that they are no longer fully operative and functioning as they were designed to. Over time, the distorted behaviour patterns further embed themselves in our psyche; we are removed from the experience of divine union.

As we awaken, the dissipated fragments of soul begin to reconnect and slowly but surely, the soul gains increasing influence in our lives. As this reconnection continues, our psychic capabilities begin to reveal themselves, tentatively at first, but then increasingly as we respond more to our intuitive inner pull to act. Where does this pull guide us? It is at this point that confusion can creep in. Sometimes by following the pull, synchronicity furnishes material 'success' in life and so in the beginning, we may feel the temptation to use the new found spiritual laws applying intention to shape the universe to yield a desired outcome. This may indeed seem to work for a while, but the underlying purpose of the universe - and that of our soul - is to create learning experiences that we may realise we are already whole and complete beyond illusionary desires or falsely perceived needs. This is true abundance; to express fully who we really and every incident conspires to help us dissolve more deeply into this sublime way of being...

"Desire is a judgment of the moment,
saying "I judge that outcome is better than this one".
It is caused by ignorance and fear,
not trusting what the universe is unfolding.
It is like applying the hand brake to a moving car,
it leads to fate rather than destiny.
Desire requires effort...
Enlightenment requires lack of all effort."
Openhand

By trying to manifest an outcome, we are denying the absolute truth of the moment. We are in effect making a statement to the universe "I am not able to accept things as they are. I am not awesomely okay with life as it is". In which case, we are IN THAT MOMENT establishing internal separation from the "All That Is". We are creating an identity which is incomplete in some way.

The soul, on the other hand, fears nothing and can locate the blessing in all situations, even those the personality may consider dark and difficult. The soul (when fully reconnected) flows fearlessly as a wave of co-creative universal activity, exploring all darkness with the untainted curiosity of a small child. Whatever the darkness, the soul will seek it out to ensure we are not attached to it; the soul is the master of circumstance, not the victim of it. We increasingly feel this awesome majesty of being as more of the soul reintegrates and infuses within us.

Our immediate destiny is Ascension (should we choose it), which can only be fulfilled by transcending our attachments and the conditioned behaviours arising from them. If we try to manifest our desires, we may create for ourselves an apparently more abundant existence in the short term. However, if this is based on materialism, or indeed any material outcome, we are likely to find ourselves attuning more to denser vibrations and less to the lighter, etheric ones of the destined, new realm beckoning us.

Ascension involves continually attuning to the higher, etheric vibrations of the universal orchestra of co-creativity. These are found in every moment by accepting the denseness - the heaviness of the base drum - but not needing to change or shape it, in which case we do not identify with it or give it energy. Instead we will locate the lightness - the subtler instruments - which transcend the heavier vibrations...

"If we want to attract lightness, we must be light;
to be light, we must be effortless;
to be effortless, we must surrender effort.
The real secret therefore, is one of surrender...
surrendering to the truth and being awesomely okay with that."
Openhand

So we are guided on a pathway of choices, each offering the opportunity to either gracefully surrender to the path, or give in to the conditioned desires of the bodymind. When we finally and completely accept that EVERY incident is being shaped by what we are being on the inside and that to struggle to manipulate or control external events is ultimately fruitless, then we are finally ready to step onto the internal super highway of guided evolution...

"The act of creating is the act of allowing.
In looking within, we see past the distortions of the ego,
to find what is meant to be.
When we know what is meant to be,
we become as one with The Divine Flow...
the inner most longing of our soul;
we become an open channel and
infinite potential is manifested through us,
and through us, the infinite cycle is complete."
Openhand

This "Realignment" happens as we surrender to the will of our soul.

The ensuing pathway soon reveals to us how EVERY SINGLE incident, event or circumstance in our lives offers the opportunity to recognise and release an attachment; where we either need a particular outcome in life or are afraid of another. It is just such circumstances that constrict us, fragment the soul and restrain our infinite liberation; they strangle the very life essence from us. This tangled web of conditioned behaviours must be dug up at the roots.

Attachments arise from temporary amnesia, where we believe that a solution in the external world will somehow render the sense of completeness, that was always already present and yet hidden under veils of illusion. When we suddenly realise the fruitlessness of trying to control circumstances we have become identified with, and instead go inwards with razor edge honesty, we will ultimately discover the root of the attachment, release it and attune instead to that aspect of wholeness and self acceptance that was already there.

However, it is not just simply the case of releasing the attachment in order to proceed. Over the years, the attachment will have built fixed neural pathways of conditioned behaviours in the brain. Just like computer software, these are programs, which once initiated, have almost irresistible cycles of action and reaction which want to be fully played out. They can be sparked off by the seemingly most trivial of things; an image, a thought, a feeling, an emotion, the chance comment of a friend or an acquaintance for example. Once activated, these holographic imprints cause the brain to unleash powerful chemicals (neuro peptides) which then flood the body's cells activating the full spectrum of emotional behaviour including pleasure, comfort, creativity, security, control, worry, fear, anger, rage, sexual urges, love, joy and the sense of contentment (just to name a few!). Through continually repetitive behaviours, we build networks of these pathways which together form an 'identity'. Written from birth by the controlling thought forms prevalent in society, we end up running inner child programs which can taint our every choice, our every taste of reality.

Each program is animated with mental imagery, emotional essences and energetic blockages forming a virtual hologram - a prison cell in which we then live. Suddenly, we are no longer acting authentically according to the soul's destined way of being and we are no longer living the lives we were born to live. Ideally, as the soul, we should be continually painting our lives on a blank canvas, where the full palette of life's rich colours arise spontaneously into form and then dissolve just as quickly. As the unfettered artist, we are meant to be totally free to create the next masterpiece of choice not limited to painting by somebody else's numbers!

So, although we may realise the root cause of our attachment, we still have to dissolve the conditioned behaviour (in other words erase the program) which is aligning us with the false path. There is one sure way of doing this: which is to confront the programs, realise where we are being influenced and then go deeply and honestly into the repetitive cycles of behaviour AS THEY ARE HAPPENING.

In that moment where we may have previously given in to the pattern, if we can pause and centre deeply within the soul, then we will be made aware of an alternative way of being; a 'gift of beingness' will be revealed to us offering an alternative choice of action, one that is more aligned with our authentic pathway. For example, instead of always unsuccessfully seeking the right words to win an argument, we might instead realise there is nothing to win and let the silence speak more profoundly than our words ever could. Paradoxically, we may find our silent, innate completeness prospers in the interaction anyway.

Or it may be that we have been living our lives to please others, afraid of speaking our truth for fear of how it may upset or harm another. Let us be clear, NO ONE can be harmed by the truth; the greatest gift we can give to another is to dispel an illusion, including one they may be holding about us. If they are living in a lie and we are sustaining that, we are helping them be dependent on something which does not exist. In my view, this is the greatest harm we can bring to another; better to help them burst their bubble and invite them to deal with reality the way it really is. In so doing, we offer them the greatest gift of life itself - an authentic choice.

It is in such circumstances as these where we begin to unleash the divine 'warrior' and 'goddess' energies arising through the soul. These can be equated to the qualities of purpose and surrender. One, the male aspect, furnishes the passion and courage to confront those issues holding us back; the other, the female aspect, invites us to be awesomely accepting of whatever is currently happening. It is this acceptance that truly enables us to experience the fullness of the moment without needing to change or pacify it. When we can be quietly surrendered, even in the moment of greatest danger, then we may notice a spark of divine, synchronistic magic calling us to act in a uniquely spontaneous way - one which completely befits the moment. If we can master the femininity of surrendered openness, we no longer fear death and therefore no longer fear life either.

The masculine in us cannot achieve this by itself. It is too insensitive to pick up the subtleties, the purpose too strong to be fully dissolved in the moment. It requires us to master the harmony between both energies...

> *"A true warrior is wise enough to know*
> *when his purpose is to surrender."*

We may stumble in the beginning, but sooner or later we realise we are not here to build some magical wonderland (it already exists!): rather we are here to unfold a way of being which is completely at one with who we really are. In this way, choices are made reflecting our highest truth. As the fixed neural pathways begin to dissolve, our soul, which has until now been fragmented and dissipated throughout the bodymind, once more begins to reintegrate within our being. It is as if we are beginning to 'reconnect the dots' so to speak.

Furthermore, as we fall into line with the orchestra of universal co-creativity, we increasingly align with the evolutionary path of our planetary system. If we summon the courage to keep walking the path of authenticity, Gateway 2 will open before us. Some call this the "baptism" because it is as if we are baptised as disciples of our soul. In other words we have reconnected and reintegrated enough of the soul to be able to attune to it on a regular basis; the soul's expansiveness becomes the driving force in our lives rather than the limiting ego. The Realignment has taken place and, whilst we will still frequently make mistakes, there remains always the underlying conviction to follow the soul's guidance. We are now very firmly aligned on the pathway leading to our Ascension through ever higher levels of consciousness. Our lives become truly magical.

Transitioning Gateway 2
-useful tools-

1. Opening the mind: *observe ourselves in all circumstances, find the lightness and natural harmony through all events.*
2. Opening the Heart Centre: *experience as much as possible of the stimulation and energy flowing through the six senses.*
3. Receive the energy of the universe: *notice an inner pull to act and follow the natural synchronistic flow of the moment.*
4. Dealing with distortions and addictive behaviour: *confront and deal with all arising distortions and addictive behaviour.*
5. Give ourselves to our highest truth: *give ourselves entirely to the right expression of our highest truth at whatever apparent personal cost.*

1. Opening the mind: *observe ourselves in all circumstances, find the lightness and natural harmony through all events.*
If we are observing ourselves as we go through life, we will witness repetitive cycles and fixed patterns of behaviour. If we are to 'open the mind' and attune more to the soul, we must notice more the experiences that generate the following types of inner sensation...

    - *completeness, wholeness and contentment;*
    - *expansiveness and timelessness;*
    - *joy, laughter and happiness;*
    - *freedom, liberation, lightness and well-being;*
    - *an inner warmth or subtle vibrations;*
    - *strong flows of purposeful and creative energy;*
    - *the feeling of complete acceptance of the moment;*
    - *when we are feeling completely at one with who we are.*

It is important to get to know intimately the activities where we recognise these sensations and allocate as much time as possible to them. It could be sitting in stillness, but it could also be exercising or dancing, walking in the countryside, listening to favourite music or taking a bath with essential oils. It might be following those experiences where we feel completely 'in the groove' so to speak. Let us be clear though: it is not just the case of taking what appears to be the soft option; for example, fasting might cause initial discomfort, but the extraordinary lightness of being arising from it might far outweigh any perceived downside. We must also watch for addictions; so drinking a glass of wine might help us feel expansive, but there are obvious detrimental side-effects if we become dependent on it to achieve the soul's natural state of openness.

Whilst following our joy, it is essential to watch and connect with our feelings. In so doing we are 'attuning' to the soul and growing its experience in our lives. We become increasingly aware that the feelings are a part of our authentic beingness already; in other words we do not have to manifest them, rather simply unveil them.

2. Opening the Heart Centre: *experience as much as possible of the stimulation and energy flowing through the six senses.*
We may define the "Heart Centre" as that aspect of the personality that is continually surrendering to the soul. If you like, it is the expanded Observer that now realises there is something much greater at work than our egotistical desires and manifestations. It is the Heart Centre that recognises we are an integral part of the overall design. It 'hears' the quiet inner voice of the soul, notices the consistency of its beingness and wishes to be completely at one with it. Although existing throughout the bodymind, it is likely that its centre is around the heart organ itself - indeed it has been shown that the heart organ's surroundings possess a vast array of neurones similar to the brain.

In order to strengthen its presence in our lives we need to open the Heart Centre further by attuning to the experiences throughout the bodymind that generate the sublime taste of divine oneness; the feelings such as lightness, expansiveness, timelessness and infinite peace that we discovered in the Awakening. So the key is to follow those experiences that give us joy as much as possible - "what makes our hearts sing" - until we are tuning in consistently throughout the day. During the experiences, we focus where appropriate on those senses that are being activated and attune individually to them by expanding their sensations in ways such as the following...

(i) **Sight:** defocus so that we see all in our field of view, especially the periphery; particularly noticing colours, shades and patterns of things.
(ii) **Hearing:** seek to hear all of the sounds in the environment, not just those that are loudest. Feel the vibrations as well as hearing them.
(iii) **Taste:** when eating, turn off all back ground activity and take the time to eat slowly, experiencing the texture of the food and chewing and tasting fully before swallowing.

(iv) Smell: take the time to smell the natural aromas of the environment, such as that of flowers, cooking food, or the natural scent of the body.

(v) Feeling: connect deeply with the feelings within the body as we do things. So whilst walking for example, how does it feel as we place our feet on the ground and transfer our body weight from one foot to the other?

As we open more to the fullness of life in this way, the mind begins to quieten its internal chatter and we feel more present, light and alive in the moment; we begin to embrace the magnificent beauty and awesome majesty of life itself. As the Heart Centre opens, our sixth sense - that of intuition - begins to strengthen. We notice more frequently how our attention is drawn to particular things. It could be a flower in bloom; the movement of a particular cloud formation; the lyrics of a favourite song. As this begins to happen, instead of struggling to interpret what they mean, we may simply ask "how does that make me feel inside?" Some signs might alert us to growing internal stress or tightness around a particular situation, others will simply be a message of love and support. Our sixth sense is now tuning us into higher benevolent guidance and its continual outpouring of unconditional love.

If we keep noticing and following, then our intuitive capability expands rapidly. We begin to build a new vocabulary with Benevolent Consciousness and the feeling that we are being looked after intensifies. A deep inner knowing takes root; everything is going to be fine, we will be guided on the right path and we will not have to face anything we cannot cope with. As this inner trust blossoms, uplifting endorphins are released into the body counteracting the programmed addictions of our cellular memory. Endorphins are like the referee levelling the playing field, ensuring we can express freely and authentically. Tension, stress, doubt, fear and worry all begin to fall away and our consciousness expands bringing us ever closer to the second Gateway.

3. Receive the energy of the universe: *notice an inner pull to act and follow the natural synchronistic flow of the moment.*
As our sixth sense strengthens, we begin to notice the natural synchronistic order of things and our inner pull to Right Action intensifies. Sometimes this pull can be felt as an energy through the Heart Centre, sometimes it is a simple inner knowing "this is what to do now". In which case it will benefit us to always respond to that pull. Where does the pull lead? It will guide us to events, circumstances and experiences that provide an opportunity to express a "divine gift of beingness" and to expose conditioned behaviour patterns formed from an attachment to a desired outcome. These are "distortions" of authentic beingness causing us to get tight, worried, angry or frustrated.

How are distortions created? For each of us, the soul is a unique harmonic of various universal characteristics (see the "7 Rays of Divine Impulse" under Gateway 3), what we may call divine gifts of beingness. These gifts are innate to the soul, but just as with children, they need much time and patience to shape and unfold the personality. If the environment in which we grow is not sufficiently supportive or evolved, distorted repetitive cycles of behaviour form (this is largely unavoidable). So for example, someone who is being controlling of people is expressing the gift of divine will (warrior energy) in a way that is trying to manipulate; perhaps the love and support they received as a growing child was conditional to them conforming to a particular type of behaviour? In other words, "you'll only get this treat if you behave". Such conditioning can generate lack of trust in the natural flow of the universe and therefore build the need in us to control events and people.

Another example is someone who is overtly self sacrificing. In this way, they are expressing the divinely feminine characteristic of surrender which has become distorted. In striving for greater harmony with others, they may disempower another by over supporting them or identifying with their illusionary problems. In so doing, they take on too much themselves thus lowering their vibration and eventually becoming depleted or washed out. In effect they are continually dissolving their own truth for the erroneously perceived benefit of another.

It is these distortions that prevent us realising our true potential in life and must be dissolved if we are to unleash the full unbridled radiance of the soul. Hence our soul guides us to confront them. In the beginning, it is frequently difficult to feel, hear or intuit our inner pull, especially if we are not used to following our natural intuition. In which case, stillness is vital to us. Rather than approaching our day with fixed ideas of what we must do, it will benefit us to spend as much time as possible "free wheeling". In other words asking the following questions and responding to the answers that arise...

Free Wheeling
(i) What is the true energy of the moment now? Seek to feel, intuit and understand what is happening in the surrounding energy field. What is my attention being drawn to? What are the underlying patterns of activity? How am I feeling right now?
(ii) What would you have me do now? Ask the universe what is the best course of action? Be still. Do not try to answer the question, just wait for awareness to flow. Observe synchronicity in the surroundings. Watch what thoughts and feelings arise, watch for an inner pull to act. It will always become clear what we are being invited to do (including doing nothing!).
(iii) Which distorted behaviour patterns are being revealed? Look for old behaviour patterns that are being exposed and identify the inner distortion. Be completely accepting of it knowing that we did not create it and it does not define who we truly are. It is merely a condition of our life's experience.
(iv) How would you have me be now?
Instead of giving in to the distortion, find and express that aspect of beingness which makes us feel more authentic, whole and complete; that which breaks limitation and feels expansive.

If we keep practising this technique of listening to and following the soul, then we will notice more and more our inherent ability to flow with the universe; it is entirely natural, but just as with any other skill, we must practice and hone it if we are to master it. The most important thing to realise is that flowing with the universe brings us directly to our distortions. So if we encounter situations where we are caused to get irritable, angry, frustrated or tight, it is not the universe having some great cosmic joke at our expense. No, we can be absolutely sure that we have made the right choices. These internal barriers are exactly the ones that need to be dissolved if we are to continue to evolve.

4. Dealing with distortions and addictive behaviour: *confront and deal with all arising distortions and addictive behaviour*
So how do we deal with the distortions? We could try to resist or conceal them by switching our attention to a more favoured reality. However, we can only avoid the truth for so long. What we resist persists and sooner or later our conditioned behaviours will reappear, although perhaps this time, in some other guise which may be even more difficult to spot.

In my experience, the key to dealing with distortions is to realise each conceals a divine gift of beingness and to ultimately unveil that instead. So, for example, someone might smoke because it gives them the feeling of relaxed completeness - this feeling is already present as a condition of our soul. We simply need to peel away the internal barriers to that experience. Here is a five step process for dealing with all types of addictive behaviour which can help greatly...

(i) Accept the distortion has a purpose: First, accept the distortion is there for a purpose which is to help us learn something about ourselves. If we contemplate this deeply and do not allow ourselves to be judged for the behaviour (everyone has similar issues of one form or another), then we find that we can be awesomely okay with the 'problem'.

(ii) Do not fight the distortion: When we are awesomely okay with something, we do not tighten around the issue and do not make it worse than it already is. So, rather than fighting the behaviour, we should experience it as much as we want to. For example, if we cannot resist eating, smoking, drinking, being angry or controlling etc. keep on doing it, be absolutely clear not to feel bad about it, but also be completely honest about the distortion.

(iii) Ask what the problem reflects about what we are being? When we are satiated with our 'fix' which each distortion fulfils, ask "what does this behaviour give me on the inside?" With anger it might be the release of frustration; with drinking it might be the feeling of confidence; with arrogance it might be self esteem. Now settle into that positive feeling which the repetitive cycle has provided, knowing that the feeling is inside of us all the time without the need of the addictive behaviour to initiate it.

(iv) Stoke the inner flame: Over time, we will discover an 'inner flame' - the soul - which begins to smoulder around the authentic feelings and becomes stronger the more we focus on them. The more we stoke the developing flame, the stronger it becomes until ultimately, we realise it is the ONLY worthwhile thing having. Then we discover that the addiction has downsides that can diminish or even extinguish this inner flame.

(v) When the flame is high enough, make the higher choice: Once we have discovered how to find the flame without any external influence and we know that the distortion ultimately extinguishes the flame, then at some point, we will be ready to give up the addiction and make the higher choice; that which has the power to make us feel good the whole time. There are likely to be many occasions before this point is reached where we give in to the addictive behaviour; be awesomely okay with that, but keep watching and being completely honest with ourselves about it. Eventually we will make the realisation that nothing can ignite our destined flame of beingness, but our own inner focus; however, the inner flame has to be high enough first in order to make that authentic choice.

The key is to remember that the experience of relaxed completeness is what we already are and all we really need to do is remove the barriers to that sublime state. If we confront the distortion, then we can release it and move through it. Avoidance simply delays the inevitable causing more suffering; the only way out is through.

5. Give ourselves to our highest truth: *give ourselves entirely to the right expression of our highest truth at whatever apparent personal cost.*
Once we have been watching our distortions for some time, we will begin to notice in each daily interaction a pregnant pause where a black and white choice is being offered before the moment is born; we either give in once more to the distortion or alternatively, express a more evolved creation - our highest truth.

Over time, we become adept at noticing this pause. Initially it can be strangled by fear. We might be afraid of the direction our highest truth appears to be taking us; to quit our job or to end a relationship or to speak out against a controlling friend or relative. Fear prevents us evolving into who we really are so, when we receive the energy of the universe, it ALWAYS guides us on a path to confront our fears. In these moments, we are being invited to express our highest truth. If fear might begin to arise and we allow it to take hold, it can permeate our consciousness and the risk is we manifest the very circumstances we fear. In such circumstances, we create an illusionary dream called the "false self" and we live out that dream. Even though false, it becomes our reality. In truth, ALL fear is illusionary and there is nothing to fear but fear itself.

To truly conquer fear is to confront it and deal with the physical, mental and emotional effects that arise because of it. In so doing, we will ultimately find a pathway through it. Here are some powerful tools to deal with fear...

(i) If fear is arising confront it: In the choice we are being invited to make, imagine the outcome we are afraid of and go deeply into it. Ask "what is the worst that could happen?" Realise that we are the eternal, which will always be unaffected by the outcome; nothing can change our inherent completeness. If we can accept this, it liberates us to be fully engaged in the moment without being consumed by negative thinking.

(ii) Breathing: When we experience fear, worry or the nervousness of desire, the chest tightens and the breathing becomes harder. It causes us to identify more with the unfolding drama. In this situation, practice deep, rhythmic breathing, bringing the energy of the universe into all areas of the body.

(iii) Tense and relax the body: In fear, worry or nervousness, the body tightens and builds negative energy which influences our every action. The best way to release this tightness is to tense and relax the parts in which we feel the tightening. This way, the stress can be dissolved and a greater level of relaxation restored.

If, in the pregnant pause before each moment is born, we can overcome our fear, then we can truly act from the Heart Centre and there is no particular outcome we need from any situation. We are simply content to be as one with the Divine. Therefore our choices are not loaded with a particular distortion or hidden desire. We are then liberated to make authentic choices in life; those that enhance and radiate our gifts.

So in overview, the approach for transitioning Gateway 2 is...

(i) open mind: be in the place of the Observer of ourselves all the time - we may call this being of "open mind";

(ii) open heart: feel all information coming in through the six senses - being always of "open heart";

(iii) receiving hand: receive the energy of the moment and respond to the inner pull to act - "receiving hand";

(iv) giving hand: pause, breathe and then give ourselves completely to our highest truth - "giving hand".

I call the approach "Openhand": living with an open mind, open heart, receiving hand and giving hand in EVERY MOMENT. Just like the message the kestrel brought to me in my Gateway 2 story, it is about keeping our focus on the moment, feeling the flow of the universe under our wings and acting unreservedly when the moment of truth beckons us.

When persistently applied, it aligns us with our true path in life. We realise our journey is an inner one where the outer world is created by unveiling what we are being within. If we continue to follow this path, although it is not at all easy, we discover we are endowed with exactly the right skills and gifts to succeed. Unfolding these gifts brings true majesty of being and boundless joy of living. To me, it is the purpose of life itself.

Transitioning Gateway 2
-general misconceptions-

1. We have attained Enlightenment: At the Awakening, the sense of release can sometimes be so powerful and so liberating that we may think we have attained Enlightenment. It may feel like there is nothing left to do. However, to be in a state of Enlightenment is to know ourselves as the Seer (pure presence) and to know this taste in and through ALL experiences ALL the time. So when we are living in a low vibrational environment, or when we are being abused and mistreated, or even in the moment of our death, can we still be coming from the place of the Seer, unattached to any of it?

2. There is no such thing as duality: As we awaken, we begin to experience the inner and outer worlds unfolding into one, we taste the consciousness uniting all things. It is at this point people frequently speak of the illusion of duality - that there is no such thing, "there is only oneness". I agree, there is only oneness throughout the universe, however oneness is expressed through multiplicity of form. If there is no "this" and "that" there would be no relativity and therefore no experience. There has to be one thing relative to another for there to be experience at all. So in enlightened states we learn to hold a divine paradox: we are being the "all of it" in any one moment and AT THE SAME TIME, we are being a unique experience of that; there is still a perceived duality even if separation is ultimately an illusion.

3. Denial of the natural flow: When we choose to, we are directed by the soul flowing to ever increasing unity through higher and higher vibrational states of consciousness. Especially where someone might erroneously think they are already fully enlightened, the mind tends to want to reject the guiding synchronicity of the soul and the inner pull to act; it can deny the natural flow through all events. This seems to be caused mostly by an unwillingness to accept the concept of perceived duality i.e. that we are whole and yet SIMULTANEOUSLY a unique expression of wholeness walking our own unique path, having our own unique experience. Or it could be that we are unwilling to accept the Divine Purpose, helping us to align with the natural harmony and flow of the universe. Since we may be unwilling to embrace this guidance, there can be a tendency to deny the flow back to unity i.e. the flow of the soul.

4. Intention led manifestation: When we begin to observe the synchronistic order of life, we begin to experience how our inner beingness is shaping and creating the events and circumstances of our outer lives. We see that when we are being tight, doubting or fearful, we manifest exactly those consequences we fear. Conversely, if we are being loving, warm and compassionate, there is a tendency to draw those experiences to us. Some call it "The Law of Attraction". However, with this realisation, there often arises the temptation to try to use the higher truth to create those circumstances we might most desire. Whilst this form of manifestation or affirmation might appear to be initially successful, its application tends to override the truth of the moment forming new layers of inner conditioning which must also be unveiled at some point in the future. It creates an identity which is non-accepting of our absolute authentic reality and disconnects us from the true path of our soul. In my experience, authentic manifestation happens as a direct result of BEING; misguided manifestation on the other hand happens as a result of what we are wanting and intending. So the key is to find out what we are really being in response to events and let authentic doing arise naturally from that.

5. Misconceived 'selfishness': It seems to be an often held misconception that it is selfish to focus on our own development when there are other people less fortunate than us who we might help instead. In my view, to truly help another is to remind them who they really are and the most powerful way to do that is to stand in our truth and shine our light as brightly as possible. Frequently, we may come across people who are in pain or suffering. If we move from our centre of awesome okayness and identify with their illusion, we continue to support that illusion by giving energy to it which is disempowering both for them and ourselves. Instead, if we continue to stay centred in our own power of beingness, there is a greater tendency to break down the illusion of suffering and help others move to that place of inner completeness themselves. It may well be selfish to focus on the individual intentions and desires of the ego, however, to me, it is most definitely not selfish to follow our heart. In so doing we align with the guiding hand of Benevolent Consciousness, the purpose of which is to awaken and enlighten all. How can this be selfish?

Transitioning Gateway 2
-signs of beginning-

Following the Awakening, it is likely that we will have experienced an extended period of at-one-ment with the universe, what some may describe as 'awesome okayness'. The illusion of separation has been, at least partially, lifted. At this point, it is understandable if the feeling arises to detach from society or at least to remain but disengage from it. However, if we continue to open, there comes a point where we begin to observe the magic of synchronicity and become aware of an inner pull to act.

When we follow this calling and act according to what we feel is right, we may notice the effects of our actions are threefold: to dispel an illusion either ourselves or another is labouring under; to 'push someone's buttons' thereby helping to reveal a distortion; or to generate a deep soul connection thereby helping to uplift, rejuvenate and enlighten. Such experiences are food for the soul and, in my experience, the more we follow them, the more uplifting it becomes for everyone.

We soon realise that is the one true purpose of the universe and to align with that purpose is to remove any internal barriers we may hold, which limit our ability to uplift both ourselves and others. When we reach this point, we are stepping onto the path, we are moving towards Gateway 2.

Specifically, we are likely to be experiencing some or many of the following...

- increasing intensity of experience through the five senses;
- noticing external events are being shaped more by our
beingness;
- the presence of divine guidance and an inner 'pull' to act;
- a change of career, relationships or life's direction;
- spontaneous 'inner knowing' and deep realisations;
- increasing intuitive and psychic capability, the sixth sense;
- increasing occurrence of synchronicity;
- noticing our actions invite an enlightening effect within others

Transitioning Gateway 2
-signs of completion-

As we step through Gateway 2, we are compelled by truth, or at least the truth as we know and feel it. It becomes increasingly difficult for us to live in a lie. If we are being untruthful or dishonest with ourselves or others, we will feel it strongly in our hearts as a movement away from peace and harmony. So we will always be feeling the inner compulsion to act in a way that expresses our highest truth.

Whilst we may not always get it right, the driving motivation is to find our authentic and genuine way of being in every moment. Consequently, more often than not, someone who has transitioned Gateway 2 will be in the place of the Observer of themselves and their motivations most of the time.

We will be responding to our inner pull and watching both the outward and inward effect of our actions. We will be familiar with the fact that all incidents are shaped to help us reveal our inner blockages and invite us to remove them. We will have become adept at dealing with those distortions. We accept fully that we are the cause of our own state of being and not to blame another if their actions appear to cause us to lose inner peace; we know we are the cause not they. In this way, we are becoming the masters of circumstance not the victims of it.

The third eye will be at least partially open, which means we will be seeing reflections of ourselves in people and circumstances. This in turn may lead to prophetic visioning and dreaming.

For someone who has undergone the Realignment, it will be our naturally arising purpose to be consciously engaged in every single moment. We will be making a constant conscious choice.

In summary then, the following are key indications we have transitioned Gateway 2...

- we are in the place of the Observer of ourselves through most events;
- we are following our inner guidance most of the time;
- the strengthening ability to interpret synchronicity;
- as the Heart Centre opens, we tend to lose judgmentalism of others;
- an increased ability to sense and feel universal life energy;
- a deep recognition of the soul in all life and a growing ability to read both our path and that of another;
- as the third eye opens, seeing ourselves reflected in others;
- prophetic dreaming and visioning;
- an inner commitment to be consciously engaged in every single moment.

Gateway 2
-summary-

After the Awakening, we may be forgiven for thinking "This is it, I've found what I'm looking for, there is no need for me to do anything else, all I have to do is to be." However, as St Augustine once said...

"If thou shouldst say it is enough, I have reached perfection
all is lost, for it is the function of perfection
to make one know one's imperfection".

So it is, when we have rested in our Awakening on the park bench of life for a while, an inner calling stirs inside, drawing us forward once more. It is the call of a long lost friend; our very own soul.

Just as the kestrel in my opening story, truth may arise as a spontaneous inner knowing, or we may feel it as an inner pull through the Heart Centre. We can no longer deny we are faced with a choice, whether to go forwards or not. An increasingly open Heart Centre, gives us the courage and strength to surrender to the inner calling of the soul. If we elect to follow, we soon discover the path is not an easy one. Whilst we may quickly realise that to effort is to take us off the path, to give up or accept 'anything-goes' is equally fruitless. A careful balance needs to be discovered; the centre path between the energies of purpose - the inner warrior - and that of surrender - the goddess of sublime femininity.

The destiny of Gateway 2 is to discover the inner harmony of the two energies; how to balance them in each circumstance. In search of this perfection, the warrior draws us fearlessly into circumstances to confront outdated patterns of behaviour; the ego is then invited to yield itself, to surrender on the altar of expanded awareness.

Where previously we may have closed down our senses in the jaws of danger, instead we are now invited to drink the moment in through every pore until we release the attachment and therefore the fear no longer imprisons us. Instead, we are liberated to express an alternative gift of divine beingness.

In so doing, we soon discover we are walking the miraculous path of co-creative activity - an harmonious symphony - where EVERY SINGLE chance happening yields a hidden code detailing the blueprint of our inherent nature. If we continue to be open and not struggle, we quickly discover we have a powerful aptitude for this new language; it is our mother tongue, the language of love. The code strips away our conditioning, unveiling who we really are.

There are many diversions on the passage through Gateway 2. The Matrix of humanity's conditioned thinking would deceive us offering new temptations, new ways to shape the drama. The promise of manifesting our dreams, but whose dreams are they? If we are not careful, we may find ourselves once more burdened by the yoke of materialistic desire. It does not even have to be the desire for a material possession or increased abundance; the allure of that as yet undiscovered soul mate for example, can send us once more into a downward tail spin. Find completeness first and that partner who is our true mirror, will simply and effortlessly arise before us.

So it is highly likely we may stray from the path and disappear off along one of life's diversionary meanderings, but with the new expanded awareness of an awakened soul, it is unlikely to be too long before we realise our progress has been retarded. In which ever blind alley we may find ourselves, we must once more become the Observer, open our minds that the Heart Centre may also fully open and receive the energy of the universe under our wings. If we can then summon the courage to give only of our highest truth, we will once more find ourselves effortlessly soaring the thermals and majestically diving into the moment of finest expression.

It is all about being finely poised, in the drama but not of the drama; fully engaged and giving of our best, but not limited or confined by the need for an outcome. It is about having the freedom from society's demands for a result, that we may flow spontaneously with the formlessness of universal consciousness and respond uniquely as the moment truly requires...

> *"The real secret is surrender... letting go to what is,*
> *because the universe has a natural design all of its own...*
> *it's continually flowing back to higher degrees*
> *of unity and oneness.*
> *And if we just let go and surrender,*
> *we can attune to that flow back like a surfer riding a wave;*
> *we don't dictate where the wave goes,*
> *we just ride it and enjoy the ride!*
> *Openhand*

When we are truly walking the path in this way, we discover it is one of divine service; service to our higher selves and to all life - there is simply no difference between the two.

In service to the One Life, we will soon discover the light of love shines with many colours. For example, to help another might be to kick away their crutch of disempowerment. However difficult this may seem at the time, eventually we unfold the strength to burst someone's illusionary bubble without fear of what the on-looking bleeding hearts might say. It is then we know with certainty, that we have stepped through Gateway 2.

The Realignment brings with it the unmistakable feeling of 'coming home'. We have now reconnected enough of the soul to feel its overwhelming inner yearning and the shift of consciousness is likely to bring us frequently to tears. We feel abundantly blessed by constant divine oversight. We are now joyfully and irrevocably embarked on the path of divine service - that which serves all.

Gateway 3
"Transfiguration"

*"Integral wisdom involves a
direct participation in every moment:
the Observer and the observed are dissolved
in the light of pure awareness,
and no mental concepts or attitudes
are present to dim that light."*
Lao Tzu

The Key: walk the path

From the author's memoirs...

For some time I had been 'walking the path', following the magical roller coaster ride of my soul. Benevolent Consciousness had miraculously provided a one bedroom flat for me on a quiet working farm in the rolling Hampshire countryside. Many joyful hours were spent connecting with the trees, the birds and natural wild life. My sensitivity to Unity Consciousness was deepening hour by hour. What had begun as sporadic acts of occasional synchronicity, was fast evolving into streaming co-creative action. As much as possible, I had abandoned mind led questions; they seemed to interfere with the natural flow of divine magic. Instead, authentic questions about the nature of reality arose spontaneously from within. When they did so, I observed they were always immediately answered. Perhaps by the movement of a particular cloud formation, the swaying of branches or the sudden darting movement of a swift. Without the constriction of mind led intention, my consciousness was directed to where it was meant to go and it became abundantly clear to me what was being said. This was the language of pure knowing, as if I had opened a direct telepathic connection to the cosmic library. When open, I would receive constant downloads of information. On the other hand, if struggling to understand or if I was trying to manifest something, the channel would be closed off instantly.

From day to day, I would simply flow from an inner pull to act, no more the restrictive limitation of a conditioned and constrained personality. I was as a surfer on a powerful wave of co-creative synchronicity. As I followed the divine flow of energy, it appeared that everything was falling into place, happening just as it was meant to. A carpet of golden light was unfolding before my feet. It quickly became clear to me that the pathway was leading to experiences exposing repetitive patterns of conditioned behaviours, which in the past had limited me. With each event, I would notice any inner tightness arising: why can it not happen this way? why is that person acting the way they are? why have I lost my sense of inner peace? I was being guided to choices and situations where I was identifying with the external drama; where perhaps I wanted something outside of myself to make me feel content, whole, loved, successful or fulfilled when all the while the only thing that could yield these prizes, was dissolving into my very own inner being; the fullness and completeness of the True Self.

At the time, I was still working in web development as the Managing Director of a fast growing company, but it was becoming increasingly difficult to take life in the Matrix seriously. With each person I encountered, I could immediately see where they were stuck, what their issues in life were and how they might unlock the inner doorways limiting them. Frequently I'd find the right key that would help people move forwards, but also encountered others who simply did not want to know; they somehow seemed content being victimised by events, continually struggling and efforting to create some illusionary prize of security, self esteem or wealth. They seemed unable to realise that it was exactly this tightness that was creating the repetitive patterns of experience in their lives; events that continually locked them into a virtual prison. I felt deep compassion for them, but in such cases I could do little. At first it created tightness in me. I wanted the whole world to wake up and see the real magic of life unfolding all around us; that beauty was not to be found in some singular separate creation - a house, a car or some big new deal - it was to be found in the miraculous weave connecting all life. I wanted everyone just to stop, breathe deeply and take a look around them, but alas, many were just not ready for that. They were too lost and I had to learn to surrender to that.

As the inner journey continued to unfold, a wonderful juxtaposition happened. I began to look forward to the moments of tightness, to the situations where I was plunged once more into the darkness, for I knew it was just a question of time before I would bob up to the surface again, to feel the brilliant warming sunlight of unconditional love. As I let go of each attachment, where I had desired a particular outcome, I experienced myself expanding outwards, unfolding my consciousness to embrace ever finer tastes of pure presence. What need had I of material manifestation, what need of approval or the acceptance of others? I was was being filled with the universe. The more I let go, the more I opened up and the more my inner emptiness was filled.

Then suddenly 'it' happened. At the time I was not sure what 'it' was, but as in my Awakening, it was just as powerful, just as earth shattering. Yet again, gaping holes were punched into the fabric I had come to know as reality. It happened on a hill top overlooking the farm where I now lived and worked. As on the roof of the Las Vegas Hilton, I found myself being washed through by wave upon wave of unconditional love, sending ripples of energy seemingly through every cell of my being. Suddenly, in a virtual inner reality, what you might call a lucid dream, the top of my head lifted off and my soul was launched skywards, rocketing into the heavens as a blazing stream of light. I departed our dense atmosphere in the seeming blink of an eye, shot through our solar system and into the unknown, marvelling wide-eyed at spectacular supernova and astral sunrises. Unbeknown to me at the time, this was the mental pictorialisation of a physical phenomenon known as a "full kundalini activation", where the consciousness that is the soul, is released from the bodymind in sufficient quantity to shoot up the spine into the pineal gland - the location of the third eye.

In the lucid dream, I found myself heading towards a black spot in the faraway cosmos - the centre of our galaxy. Even at millions of miles, I could sense its density sucking everything towards it including me. As I drew closer to the black hole, I could feel the awesome magnitude of its denseness consuming all around it. Then suddenly I was inside it, racing downwards, accelerating ever faster into this seemingly bottomless pit. In the earth shattering speed, my flesh began to ripple and then tear away, followed by bones, then thoughts, ideas and emotions, all constructs of the reality I had always known, until I became a ball of light which the immense gravitational force was now compressing and compressing until I was reduced to a super dense spark.

Then suddenly, the bottom of the abyss came into view and at its centre was a compacted sphere of super massive denseness. I accelerated even faster right towards its focal point. Fears were materialising, but there was no time for them, as they were stripped from me at the instant of arising, seemingly nothing that had any kind of substance to it could hang onto this infinite speed. Inevitably I struck it, unleashing an explosion of nuclear proportions that lit up the cosmos; the Big Bang had seemingly been re-enacted for me.

As I exploded through the bottom of the Black Hole, anything that was still material within me was instantly vaporised into nothingness leaving only peace and profound stillness. There was only oneness, infinite absolute potential, nothing arising not even an 'I'. There was oneness with everything with no separation. I had slipped through a hole in the canvas of reality and become infinite non-identified presence, the Seer of all things, the ghost in the machine. Time stood still, I was embracing eternity.

Then from nowhere the question arose "who is here to experience this?" There was no desire to answer the question for that would mean something would have to arise to create experience and any experience might shatter the stillness of this perfect nirvana. But the question had arisen from somewhere. Perhaps a wafer thin slither of mind had somehow slipped through the destruction and now wanted to own this experience for itself? Infinite stillness became a physical, material experience of bliss, something my re-emerging mind could handle. I didn't know it then, but this inner "shadow" had come to steal my absolute freedom. Then, suddenly the shadow had gone, an imposter stealing away into the night. Yet somehow I knew it had not gone, it was hidden somewhere in the far recesses of my inner universe, somewhere that could no longer be seen. The shadow was a fraudulent trickster seeking to own the radiant light of my spontaneously flowing soul, but there was no time for him right now. The material experience of bliss was too alluring. I would have to deal with him later.

Reintegration into humanity's Matrix of conditioned thinking was difficult this time. The framework of normal reference was for me completely shattered. Fragmented fixed neural pathways were no longer adequate means to express the beauty of my soul, which I was now tasting in its fullness. I could feel the essence of the Christ and Buddha Consciousness. Day-to-day existence seemed at best an irrelevance, at worst a lie; a gross distortion of truth that I could no longer entertain. Those around me, my colleagues, friends and family found great difficulty in relating to me as I now was. The old me had completely vanished, vaporised into the ether and few, if anyone who knew me, could cope with that. I had transitioned Gateway 3 and there was no going back. It was now all or nothing.

Gateway 3
-overview-

The Transfiguration is yet another powerful transition and arguably the defining moment of our spiritual unfolding. As we follow our destined pathway, we continue to reconnect with fragments of soul dissipated throughout the bodymind; the soul gains stronger and stronger influence in our lives. After a great deal of purification and soul searching, we are finally ready for the shift of inner perception from being a identity following the soul, to being the non-identifed Seer, flowing as the soul through the bodymind.

As we step into the corridor leading to Gateway 3, we are likely to experience times of great unrest and turmoil as upheaval begins to take place internally, which is often reflected externally through the circumstances of our lives. We are prone to roller coaster mood swings, one day feeling energised, invigorated and deeply spiritual and the next, perhaps tired, heavy, sombre and disconnected.

This seesaw effect is caused by internal shifts in the balance of consciousness principally through the chakras. These are etheric consciousness centres where the soul infuses into the bodymind. Put simply, it may be considered that each cell in our bodies has two different vibrations present in it. One is the heaviness and denseness of the bodymind (which we may call "Separation Consciousness"), the other is the lightness and expansiveness of the soul (which we may call "Unity Consciousness"). The chakras provide the energetic bridge - the connecting interface between the soul and bodymind.

When they are open and vibrating as designed, we experience ourselves authentically as the soul expressed through the bodymind. However, when they are closed down for some reason and their energy is convoluted, incongruent and dense, then there is a greater tendency to identify with the bodymind. It is here where we get stuck, because consciousness is not flowing freely through the chakras as it was designed to.

Due to their etheric nature, the chakra system has not yet been generally accepted within society and has been confined to the world of mysticism and spirituality. However, there is now growing acceptance - although still much disagreement - as to their exact locations and purpose. It is best therefore to use any frame of reference we may encounter, more as a guide and locate the centres through our own experience by bringing continual awareness to them. By working with them and closely monitoring the corresponding effect in our external lives, we can gauge the influence they have. I have used this approach to yield the following overview...

1. Base chakra: located around the coccyx and genitals, it relates to our connection to the physical plane including our immune system and sexuality. If the vibration here is low, we tend to be over attached and identified with the physical experience. We feel separated from the 'All That Is' and have overtly lustful and potentially exploitative sexual urges. As we transmute the energy in this chakra to the higher vibration, we are increasingly released from attachment to the physical plane and naturally aspire to higher spiritual growth.

2. Sacral chakra: located approximately where the spine and pelvis meet, the sacral chakra is the emotional centre which governs our state of being within relationships. If the vibration is low, then we tend to be overly attached in relationships, needy and jealous. As we transmute the energy and raise the vibration however, we discover increasing sensuality in relationships.

3. Solar plexus chakra: located on the spine, around the area of the top of the stomach. Its purpose is to accept and infuse higher spiritual knowing into the lower mind - what we may call subconscious mind. Indeed it can be considered to govern the correct functioning of lower mind. When the vibration is low, we are prone to mental programming and distortion and are therefore more susceptible to addictive behaviours such as attachment to caffeine, chocolate, sugar, alcohol, cigarettes and other drugs. When we fully transmute the consciousness here, we are able to take control over the base urges (of the lower animal), expand our consciousness and open up new channels of creative influence through etheric manifestation. "Telepathic Knowing Exchange" can take place from the higher realms into the Third Dimension through this chakra when functioning as it is designed.

4. Heart chakra: located at the level of the heart, this is the centre where the unconditional love for all life activates, what some call "The Christ Consciousness". When the vibration is low, it manifests as judgmentalism and the radical adherence to a singular truth, thereby precipitating conflict in our lives and limiting us to the lower Third Dimensional Realm. When the vibration here is transmuted however, judgmentalism falls away and is replaced by unconditional love for all life. We become able to see and hold multiple truths and through correct non-judgmental discernment, become able to choose Right Action in line with the guiding hand of Benevolent Consciousness (experienced as a heartfelt pull). When we attain a fully open heart chakra, we begin to unfold into the Fifth Dimension.

5. Throat chakra: located at the area of the throat, the fifth chakra connects directly to higher mind - our fifth bodily vehicle of expression (see Gateway 5). It governs our ability to receive, interpret and articulate the highest truth from the cosmic library of all knowing. The throat centre provides the doorway into higher spiritual awareness. When the vibration is low, we tend to be more bounded by the notion of separate identity, thereby limiting us more to the lower dimensions. A low vibration here would manifest as an inability to express and be at ease with authentic reality; we are governed more by the limitations of lower conditioned thinking because of our attachment to false identity. Put simply, we are less able to express our inner truth and be awesomely okay with that. The chakra opens completely when we are no longer internally affected by the outer reaction to our fully expressed truth. We are able to 'turn the other cheek' and automatically express higher wisdom at whatever apparent personal cost; thus the doorway to multi-dimensional experience is opened for us.

6. Third eye: located in the pineal gland roughly in the centre of the head at the level of the eyebrows. The third eye may be regarded as the centre of consciousness for the soul within the body. Whilst we are engaged in the transmutation of consciousness within the lower chakras, we tend to be unaware of it because our actions are governed more by the false self rather than the soul. Put simply, Soul Consciousness from the third eye is swallowed up in identification with the bodymind and its attachments to the external drama. However, as we release these attachments, the vibration in the lower chakras transmutes and then Soul Consciousness is liberated rising up the spine and reconnecting in the third eye with Unity Consciousness flowing 'downwards from the source'. This is referred to as "kundalini activation" (fully explained below). When the third eye activates, we become increasingly able to see reflections of ourselves in other people and all life. We are able to identify and align with our true sense of beingness. Thus, the soul's purpose is now being unleashed.

7. Crown chakra: located just above the fontanel where the three bone plates of the skull meet. This chakra only really activates when we have transmuted much of the density in the lower chakras and liberated enough Soul Consciousness from bodymind identification. At this point, the crown chakra opens and infuses energy into our highest bodily vehicle - the "spirit light body" (or "merkaba"). This paves the way for correct rationalisation of the multidimensional influences we are experiencing, including for example the underlying synchronistic patterning through all events. As the crown chakra fully opens, multi-dimensional living through the spirit light body becomes a reality for us. We become centred in the universal flow of Right Action and are increasingly able to shift consciousness between dimensional realms as required.

Through transmutation of the denser energies in the chakras, we are in effect becoming inner alchemists, changing the very nature of our being from lower levels of dense consciousness to higher vibrational frequencies. Allegiance is switching to the soul's lightness through each of our cells and we begin the Ascension process in earnest. We can still feel the heaviness and denseness of the physical body, but growing internal realisation consolidates that it no longer defines us. All the while, we are opening and expanding new channels, bringing in the higher energies. Ripples and waves of energy begin to flow throughout the bodymind and our consciousness expands into new dimensions of experience.

Whilst this process of internal alchemy is taking place, we become fully aware of the inner child and inner teenager acting in our lives. During the first months of life, gently cocooned in the tender warmth of our mother's womb, we probably experienced mostly unconditional love, blissful inner peace and a sense of complete at-one-ment with the universe. So much so, that when we were born, we were mostly unable to distinguish where we ended and our mother began; so complete was our sense of unity.

It is only after much initial 'education' in the ways of the world, that we begin to buy into the deception of our separateness from all life. It is then that the inner striving kicks in as we seek to acquire the things that make us feel whole once more; love, food, possessions or attention for example. Quickly, we learn which of our actions result in fulfilment and which do not; so we begin at a tender age to develop conditioned behaviours leading to fixed neural pathways in the brain.

As we continue to activate these pathways, chemicals known as neuro peptides are released by the brain (specifically the hypothalamus) into the body, generating emotional expression within our cells, thus mirroring the activity in our brain. If these patterns are continually replayed, the very nature of the cells is changed to reflect the conditioned habits. In short order, we literally BECOME the sum total of our behaviours.

Put simply, if a baby is hungry, it learns that if it cries it is likely to get fed. If the mother has a degree of stress, as is frequently the case, this will be picked up energetically which in turn becomes imprinted in our cellular memory. So a programmed loop of thought, imagery, emotion and feeling develops around getting fed. It might be for example: "I feel hungry which is not good. I don't feel complete, if I cry I'll get fed. Oh, that feels stressful and emotional, I realise that there is struggle in this place to get the things I need".

So at a tender age, we are thrust like innocent lambs into the growing pains of childhood. The driving impulse of the soul is choosing for us to explore the bountiful freedom of expression and yet, all too quickly, it bumps into the artificial boundaries of judgment, limitation and control. Of course the soul needs guidelines along which to advance, but all too often, that progression is limited, curtailed and diverted by society's small mindedness.

Resultantly, the growing infant begins to lose trust in the completeness and perfection of the universe. This new doubting forms a more stressful consciousness, mirrored and replicated throughout the billions of tiny cells forming the body (this is exactly why a simple affirmation, intention or mantra is insufficient to re-centre our consciousness).

The identification with the external drama has begun at a tender age and from that point, the separation from the divine crystallises as an inner belief system; we build more and more behavioural programs identifying with the denseness and sometimes harshness of this physical realm. The baby is learning all about pain, doubt, distrust and fear. If the parents are sufficiently evolved, they will keep reminding the growing infant to stay in the Heart Centre, keep shining the light and trust in the infinite organising power of the universe to meet our actual needs. If not, the parents are likely to be drawn into the false reality the growing infant is creating by feeding its distortions and attachments to the external drama.

At around the age of 2-4, it is likely that the neural pathways have grown to such an extent that a tangled web of conditioned behaviours has already taken root. This forms an identity - the inner child - which typically parents continue to feed; "my child doesn't eat this, behaves like that and is afraid of bees" etc. Continual weight and density is given to the identity by parents reinforcing the same conditions or by simply allowing them to persist by giving in to them.

The child continues to grow until at puberty, its bodily system surges with hormones and with that a rebellion from the constricting ways of the past can take hold. Once more however, there is a tendency to fight the external drama - the effect - rather than the internal one - the cause. The teenager discovers new types of behaviours that bring (temporary) fulfilment and so other neural networks of conditioned behaviours take shape. Very quickly a new identity develops - "the inner teenager".

These inner identities that eclipse the soul come into view by the shadows they cast, but with continued attentiveness and perseverance, we can become fully aware of them and lose our attachment by realising they do not define us. It then becomes possible to choose alternative behaviours which more accurately express our higher truth, those that the authentic child and teenager came here to express. When we step off the ever repeating treadmill, we can literally feel in our hearts which alternative approach would be more in tune with our Higher Selves and the universe as a whole. When this inner knowing is confirmed by the objective hand of synchronicity, we can trust for sure we are headed in the right direction. If we keep doing this over time, it becomes possible to heal all inner identities and dissolve them from our lives (see the tools section below for specific meditations). This leaves pure, unfettered, creative joy - the childlike innocence we were born with.

It is not all plain sailing however; if it were, the ultimate prize would not be worth having! It is typically the case, that when we have been following divine guidance successfully for some time, suddenly we seem to hit a rocky patch - a kind of brick wall - where frequently we perceive two powerful impulses seemingly leading us in two different directions. What is going on here?

Whether we know it or not, we are multidimensional beings and as such, are influenced from multiple dimensions of reality. The soul acts through the higher dimensions and when the higher chakras are at least partially open, guidance starts to flow from spontaneous knowing down into our being. This guidance is authentic, benevolent and in the interests of our highest truth. It flows into the heart chakra guiding us on the best path forwards by the rationalisation of Right Action based on non judgmental discernment. However, in order for that authentic pull to be acted on authentically, it must be seamlessly transmitted through the mind and body; in other words through the lower chakras. In so doing, it must pass through the heart chakra where we 'take charge' of the lower self. Here is where the greatest danger to authentic action lies waiting in ambush.

Hard as it may be for many to believe, there is a sophisticated life force living and acting in the Fourth Dimensional Realm all around us. Originally tasked with helping us, these entities became too identified with our evolution. They disconnected themselves from the benevolent Divine Purpose, formed their own agenda, then began to control and manipulate. To some they are known as 'fallen angels'. This "Opposing Consciousness" has become adept at stimulating our conditioned behaviours by giving energy to them. We may believe we have complete control of our thoughts, but quite often, we may find ourselves slipping into subconscious mental routines; actions which prey on our fears causing us to release emotional energy. In this way, Opposing Consciousness is actually retarding our evolution by sustaining our attachment to dense, material experience. Thus our chakras have in effect become closed down, thereby removing us from the feeling of universal peace, trust and at-one-ment with all life; in other words our divine birthright.

Within the Fourth Dimension, where Opposing Consciousness operates, it becomes possible to shape circumstances in the Third Dimension through creative intent. From my perspective, this is what is going on when awakening people speak of "manifesting" the things they want. They have opened the third chakra, expanded into the Fourth Dimension and from that higher level of consciousness, are having a strongly creative influence in the lower dimensions.

Unfortunately however, this approach has the strong tendency to generate attachment to the lower material plane - the arena of the manifestations - and it either generates a new internal identity or sustains an old one. In so doing, there is the possibility of being duped by Opposing Consciousness which might actually work with the creative intent thereby fuelling attachment and identification with the physical plane. In this way, Opposing Consciousness is able to retard our evolution thereby maintaining its source of energy. As surreal and unpleasant as it may sound, in short humanity is being farmed by this distorting influence.

So how do we combat Opposing Consciousness? The key is to first realise and accept our true purpose for being here; then to understand how our authentic impulses are being distorted. So at some point, the realisation will dawn that our central underlying purpose is not to manifest things, but to 'self realise' - to experience ourselves as what we truly are. It may be that in doing so, we end up creating things, but in authenticity, it is what we are being in the act of creating that counts and not the creation itself. So our authentic motivation is to explore beingness and if we always come from this place in all engagements, that will be a good start.

The dichotomy we must then resolve, is that in order to create we have to hold awareness of the creative act in our consciousness, otherwise the creative act might not happen. However, we need to learn how to hold this creative purpose very lightly without attachment. In my view, acts of authentic creativity tend to be spontaneous and in the moment; the impetus to act passes from higher to the lower mind and is integrated directly within our consciousness. Authentic creativity simply arises from inner knowing. We become aware of what we are meant to do and bring our thoughts and feelings to the creative act. However, if we hold the vision of a creative outcome in our minds as an intention, it becomes all too easy for that to be embellished and glamorised; all of a sudden, we become attached to the manifestation. We are taken out of the moment and start living in the future. The situation is compounded by the ability of Opposing Consciousness to mimic synchronicity as it seeks to convince us the creation itself is the most important thing.

So for example, it may be that our destined way of being is expressed as a teacher or revealer of spiritual truths and this might seem very much aligned with the creation of a particular manifestation such as a retreat centre for instance. However, it is not the retreat centre itself that counts, rather the way we are being in the creation and running of it. In other words, authentic doing arises naturally from authentic being. When we are being true to the soul, then it appears as if we are stationary and the universe is magically shaping around us. Conversely, if we are still seeking to manifest things in life, to me it is a sure sign of inner tightness and therefore a lower level of consciousness. We are being a non accepting identity, inadvertently confining ourselves to the old world reality.

Unbeknown to many in society, Opposing Consciousness has caused much confusion and deception through our energy field. By continually bombarding us with energetic stimulation and distraction, which conflict with the authentic impulses of the soul, for many people, the correct processing capacity of our lower, subconscious mind has been shut down. The solar plexus chakra is in effect no longer functioning as it was designed to; we are not able to benefit from the full power of our psychic clairvoyant, clairaudient and clairsentient skills. Consequently, it is clear that the majority are mostly unable to feel and intuit the impulses descending downwards from the higher dimensions. Instead they are acting according to the controlling thought forms prevalent in the Matrix of mass human subconsciousness. Even when they are able to perceive the impulses from their authentic higher selves, the distorting effects of Opposing Consciousness on the lower mind interferes with their ability to carry out Right Action - those choices flowing through the soul. We are unable to lead the lives we were destined to.

So at this point in our evolution, it is likely that we are experiencing two forms of guidance both appearing to be benevolent, but only one authentic. We must learn to distinguish when an inner pull is genuine and when it is a little less than the real thing. With the Observer's sharp eye and razor edge self honesty, we will ultimately sense the difference in vibration. One - the lesser - never quite feels right; it is less sophisticated, the vibration less congruent, the synchronicity less spontaneous. The other - higher benevolent guidance - is more advanced, more spontaneous, evokes deep inner longing and self knowing. We may make many mistakes, but if we are being true to ourselves, it will always become clear eventually where we stepped off the path and why. So profound self honesty and total commitment to self realisation - above all else - is the key to nullifying the distorting effects of Opposing Consciousness.

At some point, when we have dissolved enough of the distortions and are sufficiently inwardly surrendered, the internal balance of consciousness shifts positively in favour of the soul. The neural web of false identities can then suddenly shatter in the crucible of daily life. The unleashed energy of the soul rises from the base of the spine up through the body and into the third eye where it reunites with Unity Consciousness flowing down through the crown chakra. The experience can be so powerful, it may feel like the whole top of the head has just lifted off as a stream of light surges heavenward (some may also experience it in a more gentle way). Kundalini activation has occurred, often symbolised as two serpents intertwining as they rise up the spine. It is as though the phoenix of the soul has arisen from the burning ashes of identity; the inner and outer worlds unfold blissfully into one with no experience of separation. We are no longer an identity, but a flow of universal energy. The Observer has dissolved into the all encompassing Seer, like an invisible surfer riding the crest of a divine, co-creative wave.

Although beautifully profound, the experience can also be quite destabilising, particularly in a frequently judgmental world that does not generally recognise spiritual evolution. This is because although the neural webs have been shattered, the individual neural pathways are still in place as splinters of the original identity. To the transfigured being, these conditioned behaviours no longer seem appropriate as a means of expressing itself and so a sense of dislocation from the world can occur until we begin to develop more appropriate responses based on the authentic actions of the soul.

In an impatient and controlling world, it can appear that we have "lost touch", become "spaced out" or "lost the plot". In extreme cases, where the transfigured being is connecting through multiple dimensions of reality, it can seem like we are temporarily mentally unbalanced or "psychotic". It is because we are literally living in multiple realities simultaneously and initially it can be quite difficult integrating them into one overlapping and consistent experience.

Steadily however, we begin to integrate our holistic beingness and new, multidimensional experience of the universe. Initially this new integration is very demanding and physically tiring; we have connected dozens more channels of incoming information in one fell swoop, placing huge demands on the bodymind as it struggles to cope with the tidal wave of new feelings, experiences and emotions. Eventually, the experience settles down, we become adept at living in pure presence and embrace the new intuitive and psychic powers the Transfiguration has unleashed. Just as with the other transitions, our passage through Gateway 3 is likely to be marked by some noteworthy, perhaps dramatic, external event - a ceremony - as the fledgling transfigured soul comes of age.

At this point, we are now completely walking a spiritual path with a growing sense of our life's purpose during this incarnation. We will have a very strong motivation towards selfless service and be feeling the guiding hand of Benevolent Consciousness frequently through our lives. Surrendering all individual aspiration and desire, we become an executive instrument of the Divine Purpose.

Transitioning Gateway 3
-useful tools-

1. Raise energetic vibration: *cleanse and detoxify mind, body and living environment. Harmonise with Mother Earth.*
2. Dissolve inner identities: *become acquainted with inner identity filters which distort authentic expression. Disassociate from them and dissolve them.*
3. Release restrictive relationships: *cut the ties of old relationships which serve only to draw our consciousness back into former realities.*
4. Forgive both others and ourselves: *energetically confront those who may have mistreated us and forgive them. Forgive ourselves for past transgressions.*
5. Develop strong spiritual practices: *continually raise vibration and transmute the old consciousness. Open the chakras further, activate kundalini.*

1. Raise energetic vibration: *cleanse and detoxify mind, body and living environment. Harmonise with Mother Earth.*
The Transfiguration is an internal shift of perception from identification with the denseness and general tightness of the bodymind (experienced as a subtle inner efforting), to the non-identified, crystal clear clarity of the Seer, flowing as the lightness, expansiveness and timelessness of the soul. It is as if we are the conductor of an orchestra, in which our attention has for too long been focussed on the brass section and base drum because they were making the most noise. To hear the finer, quieter instruments, we must first turn down the noise of the louder ones.

So the key is to quieten down internal activity. This can be achieved by regulating the denseness of vibrations we bring into the body, thereby limiting the stimuli that raise our internal metabolic rate. So for example, if we eat dense, processed foods polluted with toxins, then the body has to work harder to process them and the extra effort swallows up consciousness. In other words, we get lost in the dense vibrations. Or if we pollute our minds with negativity, such as that caused by the judgmentalism frequently expressed on the TV, in newspapers and through other media, then we tend to tighten inside. Internal tightness is also heightened by too much computer time, over use of electrical gadgets and chemical toxins used in household cleaning materials. The key is to change our immediate living environment to raise our energetic vibration - to attune to the finer instruments in the orchestra. Here is a brief summary of the changes we can undertake to raise our vibration...

- *declutter our living environment;*
- *reduce the number of electrical gadgets used;*
- *get rid of the TV or be more selective about its use;*
- *avoid judgmental press and media;*
- *reduce usage of mobile phones and wireless internet;*
- *use natural cleaning products for the body and environment;*
- *wear natural clothing such as cotton, linen, hemp, silk and wool;*
- *eat less processed foods and switch to vegetarian or vegan diet;*
- *fast regularly to speed detoxification;*
- *meditate regularly to calm mind and emotions.*

We are also likely to find that it becomes increasingly difficult to use certain language with negative connotations. Words become of great significance as we realise their energetic power. There may be particular word associations with our old behaviours that we may wish to avoid using, or swear words that conjure emotions of our previous consciousness. The use of sexual swear words can be particularly self defeating, dragging us back into the realm of judgmentalism, manipulation, lack of respect and projectionism.

Other words also generate internal tightness thereby swallowing our consciousness and once more constricting our experience of our newly expanding reality. For example, I have found the word "hate" to be particularly negative. So the key is to notice the effect of the words we use and decide which we should discard from our daily vocabulary.

We will inevitably discover that this purification activity brings us into greater harmony with Mother Earth and her natural ecosystems. We find that it becomes increasingly difficult to damage, pollute or act carelessly with regard to the environment. As we become more compassionate in our approach, we are naturally attuning to the Soul of the Earth, bringing with it great joy and rejuvenation. It is as if the animals are talking to us, birds singing for us and the wind uplifting us. The more respectful and in touch we become, the more our psychic and intuitive capacity expands with synchronicity speaking to us through the weave of events.

2. Dissolve inner identities: *become acquainted with inner identity filters which distort authentic expression. Disassociate from them and dissolve them.*
The inner child is not to be confused with the natural joy, inquisitiveness and innocence inherent in the soul. It is a complex web of fixed neural pathways in the brain which typically forms between the ages of 2-4 in response to repetitive patterns of activity in our immediate environment. It is this web that becomes our initial personality which we tend to identify with.

As we grow and are subjected to other life changing circumstances such as puberty, new patterns form which create other neural webs such as the inner teenager (typically forming between the ages of 12-16). These tangled webs of complex behaviours and beliefs integrate to form identities - what we may call the false self. It is these filters which distort and dilute our absolute authentic taste of reality, generating false and unfulfilling lifestyles.

To be transfigured, in other words to dissolve into the Seer and unleash authentic beingness, we must break apart these complex webs and liberate ourselves completely from them. In other words, we must heal and dissolve the inner child, the inner teenager and any other personality filter that has evolved over time. Here is a powerful meditative technique for achieving this...

Personality healing meditation

- If possible acquire a picture of yourself both as a child between the ages of 2-4 and as a teenager between the ages of 12-16. If no pictures are available, simply visualise yourself as closely as you can at these times.

- Set aside some free time and sit quietly in a still room with candle light, incense and soft music. Connect first with the inner child. You may be able to locate the feeling of it somewhere in your body. If not, simply rest with a vision or maybe the sound or words of the child. Build up an accurate picture of your experiences. What behaviours did you exhibit? How did you feel? How were your parents towards you? What activities caused you pain? Which activities gave you joy? Build a general feeling of your personality at these times.

- When you have built up as much feeling and connection with the child as you can, simply rest in awareness of it, whatever may be arising for you including sadness and pain.

- Next connect with the inner teenager. As before, build up a picture of your experiences. What were you frequently feeling? What was your general state of mind? How were your interactions with your friends, family and teachers etc.? What behaviours did you exhibit? What gave you joy, liberation and feelings of completeness? When did you get tight, depressed or lacking in self confidence? Get to know all these things and build as complete an internal picture as you can.

- Now locate where the teenager is within you. Invite the teenager to connect with the Child recognising that they are both interconnected; one was formed in response to the other.

- Project out from yourself both the inner child and teenager (plus any other identities you may feel have formed). Have them sitting before you. First know yourself as not them. Whatever suffering has been generated, it is not you that is suffering. Settle into the realisation that you are already free from them.

- Next, through your thoughts, invite both personalities to forgive those who might have caused the pain, suffering or conditioned behaviours to form. Help them realise it was not the fault of parents, friends or adversaries, for they too were all conditioned by society.

- Once you feel the personalities have been able to forgive, focus on healing. Visualise powerful golden healing light bathing the personalities in front of you. See them surrendering into the light, healing and steadily dissolving.

- Once you have finished the session, bring the personalities back inside you again, but know they are now less impactful on your life because they feel they have received the loving attention they require. Keep performing the meditation and notice over time the personalities are becoming more content, healed and increasingly transparent, until at some point they disappear completely.

3. Release restrictive relationships: *cut the ties of old relationships which serve only to draw our consciousness back into former realities.*

During the Transfiguration, our perception of reality will shift dramatically and it helps to provide fertile ground for the new internal perspective to take shape. Constant reminders of who we once were by unsupportive friends and family, simply serve to give energy to the old patterns of behaviour. It is likely that many of the people we have grown up with, will want to keep relating to the false self they have known over the years. Frequently, their expectations may cause us to act and behave in the old predictable ways. It is as if their consciousness keeps dragging us back to the former reality. As painful as it may initially be, it will serve us to move away from this limiting energy, at least temporarily.

Leading up to the Transfiguration, we have relied on these fixed patterns and relationships with the world to provide the security of an identity we thought we needed. As the tenets of that identity start getting stripped away however, it can be deeply unsettling for those around us, as they try to hang on to the way we once were. Humour, sarcasm, judgmentalism and projectionism are frequently used, albeit subconsciously, to tie us into that state of behaviour they are most comfortable with.

This activity can seriously hamper our unfolding as we keep getting swallowed back into the old identities and patterns. At this point, it is important to be absolutely clear with ourselves what our objective is; is it to move forward into the new state of beingness being offered to us? Or do we prefer to linger in the past?

How ever long we labour in this dilemma, it will ultimately become clear to us that the only way out is forwards. At this point, it will help us to be profoundly honest with ourselves about which of the old relationships still serve us and which do not. Are we maintaining them purely out of perceived responsibility? Or perhaps it is nostalgia for that almost, but not quite forgotten taste of a bygone time? If we simply ask the question of the universe:

"Which relationships no longer serve me?"

it will become abundantly clear through synchronicity which we are being invited to release and how to do it. Whilst tact helps avoid unnecessary pain, honesty is the sure route to cutting the ties restricting our unfolding gifts of beingness.

We may find however, it is not sufficient just to break off the relationship itself. An energetic body will have formed linking both parties and to which both will now be relating. Hence we must also cut the interconnecting lines of energy. This is where honesty is so important. If we are clear to our former friend exactly where we stand and that it is time to move on, then they will be left in no doubt and the relationship can be ended as painlessly as possible. Furthermore, it is likely that the energetic bonds will be severed at that point. If not, they may continue well after the relationship has (on the surface) ended. If this is the case, it is possible that we will still be influenced by the old consciousness and it may limit our freedom to unfold.

If we sense this is happening, the following meditation can help solve the issue...

Cutting old ties meditation
- Choose a room which is open and clear. Use natural lighting and burn incense. Play gentle and healing music.
- Settle into relaxed, deep breathing.
- Visualise the person you wish to release and then connect with their soul. Visualise both of you at a crossroads.
- Inwardly thank your friend for their involvement in your life and the valuable lessons they have brought. Acknowledge it is now time to walk separate paths. Be absolutely clear with one another your paths are now moving in different directions.
- Hug lovingly and release each other. Watch as your friend takes the alternative route. Wave and wish them well.
- Before you embark down your path, visualise a tree branch in your hand and use it to brush away any remaining strands of connection.
- Visualise/feel your energy field being clear and unrestricted. Walk freely down your new pathway.

Even with those relationships we feel it important to retain - with parents for example - it will still pay to create greater breathing space for us to unfold. So it might help to move, at least temporarily, to a place of relative seclusion; where like minded people might be more readily accessible - such as a retreat centre or spiritual community for example.

In this new place of greater openness, we can begin to develop closer connections with our soul family, who are providing assistance from the higher realms. To initiate this, all we really need to do, is to know they are there, open our hearts and invite in their help. Then by noticing arising synchronicities, we know we are being answered and begin to build up an expanding picture of their benevolent involvement.

4. Forgive both others and ourselves: *energetically confront those who may have mistreated us and forgive them. Forgive ourselves for past transgressions.*
The purpose of all experience is self realisation; to know ourselves as complete and whole without fear, doubt or suffering. The only way to know hot is by first knowing cold, so to truly know ourselves as unconditional love beyond all suffering, we must first suffer and release ourselves from our suffering.

It is my view that before each incarnation, we agree with other souls that we will come together in particular circumstances to give each other the experiences we need in order to liberate ourselves from the illusion. If we each look back through our lives, I am sure we will see how exactly the right person showed up at exactly the right time to teach us something we needed to learn.

Some of those experiences will be joyous ones, others painful. Another soul may be at a lower vibration to such an extent, that they forget themselves and in so doing, carry out some action which causes pain or suffering to us. No matter how it may seem at the time, the Divine Purpose is to provide an opportunity for us to learn and evolve; to find the place where we are unaffected by it. In this way, everything we may consider as negative action perpetrated against us can actually be perceived as a blessing. When someone pushes our buttons or causes an emotional stir, we have been given a gift; the opportunity for liberation and thereby expansion. Remember, to be enlightened is to be enlightened by all things.

When we truly realise and accept this, we have the possibility to be released from the pain and suffering of all negative actions that have been carried out against us, including judgmentalism, emotional and physical violence, slander or abuse. When we go deeply into such transgressions, we find our sense of lack actually drew the circumstance to us in the first place. Maybe for example we needed someone to be loving or behave in a particular way? Maybe we needed them to be kind and not hurtful? In these circumstances, we were looking outside of ourselves for something we already possessed within. No one can take our energy or inner peace, we can only give it away. No one can judge us; it is we who allow ourselves to be judged. In which case, we are really judging ourselves.

In the state of Enlightenment beckoning us all, we and we alone, are the creators and therefore masters of our experience of beingness. To take back our true majesty and power in life, is to take back the blame for anything we experience; in other words, to acknowledge ourselves as the creator and then to own our creations.

From this perspective, we need to find another way of looking at forgiveness in terms of how it is traditionally understood. True forgiveness is to find awesome acceptance of what occurred and embrace the perpetrator as an instrument to help us unfold. We are all evolving and at the soul level, we manifest co-creative events to provide opportunities for growth. To me, true forgiveness therefore is to see the blessing and find that place within, where we are at peace with the issue. It is not an easy internal transition to make, but when we can truly liberate ourselves from projecting blame or taking on blame, we find it much easier to forgive and be forgiven. If we can find awesome acceptance, then we discover a new level of internal freedom. We are no longer held prisoner by events of the past.

Here then is an appropriate forgiveness meditation to help us release inner tightness caused by events where we believe negative acts have been perpetrated against us...

Forgiving another meditation

- Create a loving, warm and protected space with incense, candles and soft music. Relax deeply using deep breathing and visualisation.

- Allow an experience to arise in the past where you have suffered or were abused at the hands of someone else.

- Contemplate deeply the situation where you suffered, visualising what you would have seen, hearing the sounds and feeling the feelings.

- What thoughts and emotions are arising for you? Watch them, feel them.

- Go deeper into the situation and contemplate the main perpetrator/s. What was it that caused you to suffer? What were you attached to? How were you forgetting this is all an illusion?

- Now contemplate what was the blessing? What was the lesson? What were you being invited to realise?

- Can you now let go of the suffering and pain?

- When you know you are ready, feel the darkness gathering into a heavy, dense ball in your right hand and then next see the ball dissolving into light.

- Now visualise the perpetrator. Connect with the soul in them. See firstly their perfected light.

- Can you now let go of your resentment, fear or hate? Can you release yourself from judgment?

- Keep working at it until you can let go of all such negativity.

It is also important to release ourselves from our own self judgments about actions we may have carried out against another. We are not to blame! Just as in the above example, it is important to realise that due to our state of evolution, we took on a particular distortion and lower vibration, causing us to behave in a certain way. This in turn generated an experience of pain in someone else, inviting them to learn and evolve. Another way to look at it, is that our karma has created the situation and therefore once again, realise we are not to blame.

Whilst we may not be to blame, we are still responsible for the action and for releasing the distortion and lower vibration which caused it. Therefore it is important once more to confront the action and see where we were stuck. It is only then that we may be able to release any pent up frustration and self judgment. In other words, we become able to correct the outdated pattern of behaviour which no longer serves us. Here is a meditation for self forgiveness...

Self forgiveness meditation
- Create a loving, warm and protected space with incense, candles and soft music. Relax deeply into breathing and visualisation.
- Contemplate where you have hurt another either physically, emotionally or psychologically.
- Where might you have been deceitful or untrustworthy?
- Where might you have slandered or spoken badly of another?
- Where have you judged other people?
- Where have you polluted Mother Earth or hurt animals or plants?
- Go deeply into the situations, accepting that whilst it is your responsibility for what took place, you are not to blame; each action invites self realisation by the whole.
- Realise your own distortion, perhaps where you were lacking trust or respect or where you might have felt the compulsion to control due to self doubt, a sense of lack or fear.
- Resolve with yourself and those who suffered as a result of your actions, to release your distortions and raise your vibration.
- Help them to heal by bringing loving golden light to them.
- Finally release yourself from self judgment. Know that you are always embraced and loved unconditionally by your guides, soul family and even those who suffered from your actions.
- Feel all the darkness, pain and suffering within gathering into the left hand. Watch it form a dense ball which is then dissolved into light. Feel a new sense of lightness wash over you.
- Keep doing this until you have completely forgiven yourself for all perceived transgressions.

5. Develop strong spiritual practices: *continually raise vibration and transmute the old consciousness. Open the chakras further, activate kundalini.*

By now it is likely that we will have acquired meditative practices which we conduct on a daily basis (remember meditation is where we are being in conscious awareness of ourselves and surroundings and this can be achieved in many ways not just the formal meditational arts). It is not within the scope of this book to go into the various specific practices. The key is to always follow our heart and it will become abundantly clear which practices work best for us; whether it be sitting in stillness, yoga, tai chi, dancing, singing, chanting, performing the martial arts, simply walking in nature, or something else.

One of the key things to remember, is that we are all unique and have a unique pathway to Enlightenment (even though we may pass through the same milestones - the same Gateways). So whilst we may resonate with one particular practice or another, it is likely that only specific aspects of that discipline are of true value to us. It is highly recommended therefore, that we be open to developing our own daily practice, allowing it to continually evolve as we become increasingly sensitive to our unfolding inner state of consciousness.

When the Transfiguration occurs, it does so with a kundalini activation. As already described, This is where waves of Soul Consciousness are liberated from bodymind identification, flowing upwards from the base of the spine, connecting the chakras and reuniting with Unity Consciousness flowing downward through the crown chakra. The two energies then meet with a glorious explosion of light in the pineal gland - the third eye. Suddenly, we are reconnected with the cosmic library of all knowing, becoming at one with all things and powerful new energies descend over us. It is at this point, we are truly being our higher selves and by grounding that energy in this realm through the lower chakras, we become a focal point for co-creative universal activity.

Kundalini activation should occur naturally as we remove the energetic blockages, attachments and distortions from our life. However, the movement to Transfiguration and full kundalini awakening can be accelerated by performing particular spiritual practices including breathing into the chakras, singing or humming into them, using colour, sound or crystal therapy. Below is a suggested breathing meditation inspired by Kriya Yoga which I have found particularly powerful...

Kundalini activation meditation

- *Take a few deep breaths inhaling into the area of the eighth chakra several inches above the crown.*
- *Now inhale into the eighth chakra, hold the breath, then move attention down to the crown chakra and exhale into the front of it.*
- *Hold the breath on exhale and feel a sense of release, opening and expansion. You can visualise to help, so perhaps see a flower opening or a sun coming up or ripples flowing outwards on a pond.*
- *When you naturally feel it is time to inhale again, move the attention through and out of the back of the crown chakra and once more up to the eighth. Inhale into the eighth chakra. When fully inhaled, hold the breath and move attention to the third eye entering it through the front. Exhale and release tension and effort as before and then once more inhale back up to the eighth.*
- *Continue the process down through each chakra to the base and then repeat the sequence in reverse upwards beginning with the base (so we open the base chakra twice in succession). Remember, we always inhale into the eighth chakra and then exhale into the chakra we are opening.*
- *When complete, attune to the rise of energy from the base chakra up through the other chakras stopping at the third eye; feel yourself drawing the energy upwards with sense of purpose.*
- *If the energy gets stuck in a certain chakra, keep exhaling into it and releasing tension and effort there. It is likely you will need to repeat this over weeks and months to fully unleash the flow.*

It is important to state that we cannot simply raise our energetic vibration by opening and cleansing the chakras through healing practices and meditation. What actually happens, is that our work shines the light into those areas we most need to develop next, or are naturally ripe for development. In other words, that aspect of consciousness which is now wanting to unfold, will be 'spiked' in some way. In so doing, the inner blockages - the convolution of consciousness - will project into our outer world creating patterns of repetitive actions and behaviour; cloudiness in the river of life through which we now must penetrate. We are then invited to unravel our highest truth within those engagements just as before.

So for example, if we bring our attention to the sacral chakra and raise the vibration by releasing tension and effort there, we will notice the effects the shift of consciousness is having in our relationships. Past patterns of limiting behaviour (over attachment and neediness for example) will be brought to the surface and ignited so we can see them. We then have the opportunity to let go of that particular counterproductive behaviour; in so doing the consciousness in the sacral chakra rises to a more evolved state.

Thus meditation and spiritual practice can help initiate this action, but it is no substitute for self realisation in day-to-day life. Although for example kundalini activation meditations can open up our chakras, in my experience, full kundalini awakening will not happen until we have cleansed away much of our distorted behaviour patterns. We have to be very clear internally to attune to our higher self and infuse it more fully into our lives.

As we release tension and cleanse the chakras, our consciousness begins to transmute to the higher vibration. This causes a reflection outwards and the manifestation in our lives of authentic soulful action - Right Action. This does not necessarily always result in Right Outcome (that aligned to the divine flow), but at least the stimulus of the soul is being amplified making it easier to follow.

Whilst we are conducting this work, it will also be of profound benefit for us to engage in some form of psychic protection to nullify the interfering effects of Opposing Consciousness. As we cleanse internally and connect more with our higher selves, we are now lighting up in the higher dimensions and can draw negative energy to us just like moths to car headlights.

At this point, some speak of closing down the chakras and to form a protective bubble. However, in my experience, this is counterproductive to our evolutionary destiny. We are actually playing into the hands of that energy wanting to make us fearful and thereby retarding our progression. There is nothing to fear from Opposing Consciousness but our fear itself. The key is to 'become as nothing' in it all. To find the place of emptiness and clarity which can feel the negative energy, have it wash through us, and yet remain unperturbed by it. Here then are some key considerations...

Countering psychic attack

- Increase the vibrationary state of our living environment. This could involve establishing energetic and/or crystal 'grids'.
- Continually cleanse and evolve the chakra system especially from the solar plexus down.
- Become the Observer and in particular monitor motivation for decision making; let all decision making flow according to our perception of our highest truth.
- Become 'nothing in it all'. In other words, monitor internal experience and release physical tightness, together with any emotional or mental attachment to perceived psychic attack. Prevent tightness from arising within.
- If we do perceive the inflow of negative energy through the solar plexus (experienced as tightness or "butterflies in the stomach"), we may envisage a glowing ball of light within the chakra burning away any distorting influence.
- Project positive creative intent outwards from the solar plexus.
- Invite in the protective assistance of Benevolent Consciousness.

Transitioning Gateway 3
-general misconceptions-

1. Discernment disappears with judgment

As the Heart Centre opens, our experience of Unity Consciousness expands profoundly. We are instinctively able to connect with the soul in all things. Even if another is being judgmental, aggressive, rude or hurtful, we are able to perceive their soul, their distortion of it and understand why and how it has likely happened. We become able to see multiple truths in all circumstances without the need to hold one particular truth. Hence, it becomes easier and easier to dissolve judgment of others for their behaviours and actions. However, while there is still some identification with the bodymind identity, there is still the tendency to distort these truthful inner impulses of the soul. So we - as the false self - can tend to exaggerate this experience of non-judgmentalism and abandon even proper discernment. It is important that as we unfold, we are able to accurately discern the state of another, in order that we may better help or even avoid helping all together, if the engagement were likely to be fruitless. This calls upon us to hone our powers of non-judgmental discernment.

2. That we have to dissolve the personality

As the third eye opens, we are more able to see our true reflection in all things and of course especially in people. We begin to know which aspects of our nature are being revealed to us. As we dissolve away distorted layers, the edges of apparent duality become increasingly blurred as we seem to expand into everything. We become so filled with the taste of oneness and the perfection through all, that individual personality may seem superfluous (to a degree) and a kind of aloofness can arise beyond the confines of personality altogether. At this point, a common misconception can arise that we are moving to a point where personality is not necessary at all, or if it is, that it is somehow a monotone Buddha or Christ-like uniformity. In Enlightenment, we each retain a personality, it is just that we are no longer identified with it and our conditioned neural pathways have been removed. So moving into Enlightenment is not about dissolving the personality, even if it is a very powerful and imposing one. Authentic personality is all about allowing authentic expression of the soul to shine undimmed through the bodily vehicles of expression.

3. That we must be completely pure

On the path to Gateway 3, there is a strong natural pull to cleanse and purify the bodymind. This allows the internal metabolism to quieten, in order that we may identify less with the realm of the material and more with that of the spiritual. It is entirely right and necessary that we raise our vibration in this way to facilitate the Transfiguration. However, the false self tends to own all authentic inner pulls at this point to some degree or other. So at this point, there can be a tendency to think we must resist any course of action that would take us back into density. Thus there frequently develops an attachment to purity. To be in a state of full Enlightenment is to be enlightened by all things. This means to be able to experience darkness, have it flow through us, even lower our vibration (perhaps in order to serve) and yet still know ourselves as the unattached, non-identified Seer of all things.

4. That we must remove ourselves from society

Whilst it can be profoundly beneficial to take a break from time to time (a retreat away from negative influences), it is a misconception that we must completely remove ourselves from society altogether. It is in within our daily interactions with people and life's myriad mosaic, which reveals where blockages and restrictions to our evolutionary unfolding occur. In fact, it is difficult to see how we might completely remove our distortions without confronting them.

Perhaps the situation is different for someone like a yogi for example, who may have always lived in an environment free from distorting influences; however, for those of us who have been exposed over many years to society's conditioning, by far the best way to release those patterns is by confronting them. Courses and self realisation programs can help reveal certain blockages such as our inner child or past life issues, or they may teach powerful spiritual transformation practices, but ultimately, it is the application of these realisations in everyday life where true evolutionary progress is made.

5. That we must stick rigidly to a particular practice
The key to our spiritual unfolding is to listen to the quiet voice within and to follow that moment by moment. Particular spiritual practices can greatly enhance our ability to listen, tune in and follow. However, sometimes these practices can become over disciplined and dogmatic (similar to an overly restrictive religion). If we listen to the inner voice, it will tell us exactly what we need to do to enhance our unfolding. It is likely that we may wish to meditate (in the formal sense) at particular times of the day; however, if we religiously follow a fixed schedule or program, the mental intention simply overrides the natural spontaneity of the soul which is seeking to unveil a unique expression in every moment. So we are likely to find that if we are truly following the soul, our practices for enhancing that soul integration will be varied and continually evolving. From my perspective, when we are being truly authentic, dogmatic discipline is replaced by a continually evolving and enhancing rhythm of natural flowing spontaneity.

Transitioning Gateway 3
-signs of beginning-

The lead up to the Transfiguration is not an easy one. Our passions are being tested in the fullest so that we may determine what is a truly authentic expression of the soul and on the other hand, what are the mental distortions causing us to want to 'own' those expressions. So we may feel to express absolute joy of living and then find that we are attached to life itself; we may feel profound love for another, but then want to control them; we may feel the pull to completely surrender from the drama of society and then discover ourselves being listless and lacking purpose. All such experiences are designed to help us resolve out and transmute the lower behaviours - the denser consciousness.

There is no short cutting the process of transformation. It requires much dedication, perseverance and persistence. There is no magic wand that can be waved, the only way out is through. Knowing our pathway is not enough, we must also walk it. We make choices and then seek to understand with profound self honesty why we made that particular choice. Was it because of a lower base human instinct or conditioning? Or was it a genuine pull to express higher truth both for our own good and the good of all life?

If we are in a place where we are continually seeing and contemplating the bigger picture through all our choices in life, then this a good indication that we are advancing towards the Transfiguration. Specifically we are likely to be experiencing some or all of the following...

- a roller coaster ride of emotions, thoughts and feelings where one day we might feel energised and high, but the next might be confusion and depression;
- headaches as the third eye and crown chakras begin to open;
- confronting patterns of behaviour emanating from old identities;
- increasing observation of synchronicity;
- increasing psychic and intuitive capability;
- expansion of consciousness resulting in multidimensional experiences including deep revelations as to the nature of reality;
- Opposing Consciousness derailing us from our true pathway;
- destabilising sense of perception as consciousness shift occurs;
- difficulty in communication and right expression.

Transitioning Gateway 3
-signs of completion-

The Transfiguration is perhaps the most profoundly beautiful of all. It is where we know ourselves as what we true are - the Seer - experienced as pure presence. We will know beyond a shadow of a doubt our inviolable connection with Unity Consciousness and that our soul is a unique expression arising from that.

We will have tasted the profound joy of full kundalini activation - a deep recognition and reconnection to the whole of life, experienced through every cell of our being. The mere contemplation of Mother Nature's simplicity, a tree, a leaf, a flower might be enough to reduce one to tears as the shocking recognition of the true meaning of life comes into focus. Not only do we sense the interconnectedness of all life, but now we feel it in every cell of our being.

It becomes practically impossible to damage, pollute or exploit any sentient life form unless it is clear beyond all doubt that it is in their higher interests and that of all life. As the energy of the soul reintegrates and infuses within our being, we experience enormous surges of energy, heat, light and super consciousness. In summary, we are likely to experience some or all of the following...

- full kundalini activation will have occurred and experienced perhaps as profound bliss or indescribable joy;
- kundalini activation may have been accompanied by powerful lucid dream experiences;
- we will have tasted the experience of the non-identified Seer as an all embracing sense of universal presence;
- the pull and characteristics of our soul will be felt within, although we might not necessarily be able to define its qualities;
- friends and family will notice that our personality seems to have changed quite dramatically;
- we are likely to appear very relaxed, non attached and calm;
- there is likely to be a strong inner motivation to serve humanity;
- feelings of complete at-one-ment with the universe.

Gateway 3
-summary-

Imagine the experience of everything being stripped away; everything we thought was real, every belief, thought and emotion. Imagine the building blocks of a reality founded on the idea of separation being mercilessly obliterated. Imagine the very tissue of our paper thin reality being shredded to pieces in the blink of an eye. Now imagine even that which can contemplate such things - that which questions and perceives answers - also being obliterated leaving only pure unadulterated presence.

Impossible to imagine? Indeed it is, for the Transfiguration can ONLY be experienced. Words, books, poems and texts have been written through the ages about this glorious state of non-identified presence, that which miraculously arises like the mythical Phoenix from the ashes. Although some great poets might find something approaching acceptable eloquence, even they fail to convey the extraordinary flavour that can only be tasted with our own lips.

So what is the value of discussing it at all? We are transitioning very turbulent times and currently society in general has negligible understanding or tolerance for those who might experience temporary dislocation and destabilisation as the Transfiguration kicks in. For some, the Transfiguration can be a very smooth, even a gentle transition, but for others it will be earth shattering. Where the sense of dislocation is intense, health service help might be sought. Unfortunately, all too often, mental instability or even "psychosis" is diagnosed and drug induced 'corrective' treatment prescribed when all that is really required, is to allow the new consciousness to integrate in a nurturing and gently supportive environment.

Although we cannot know exactly when the transition is going to happen, it pays to be aware when we are approaching the Gateway and to be open to changing the circumstances of our environment to accommodate it. Perhaps it might be best to spend time at a retreat centre? Perhaps we can connect with a spiritual teacher who understands the process? At the very least, it would be wise to involve a close friend and explain to them what we feel is happening and that we may need to contact them at short notice for support.

Following the Transfiguration, the way we experience life changes radically. Finally, there is the knowing that all our life's experiences are manifested from what we are being within and are designed to reveal something to us. Intuitively we know the answers to all arising questions. Whilst we may choose to work with a guide, the only acceptable ones are those evolved enough to act knowingly as a mirror, either reflecting our beingness or our distortions...

"Do not believe anything because it is said by an authority,
or if it is said to come from angels,
or from Gods or from an inspired source.
Believe it only if you have explored it
in your own heart and mind and body
and found it to be true.
Work out your own path, through diligence."
Guatama Buddha

Paradoxically, since we have now stopped seeking, everything we need to do in the rest of our lives begins to unfold before us. For the first time, we are likely to get an accurate insight into our heavenly purpose here on Earth. Perhaps it is to help Benevolent Consciousness by harnessing the new energies? Perhaps it is to help cleanse Gaia's field? Maybe it is to help people overcome their own barriers and blockages? Or it could be to help maintain a degree of stability and sustainability whilst more people step onto the internal super highway that is our Ascension...

"In the beginning there appears to be
endless choice of direction,
with the course being set by the ego.
After a while it becomes clear that all the time
we have been following a destined path,
a path that leads to a way...
for each, a unique way of being.
And once we have found that way,
we discover choice once more...
either to follow the way or not.
If we choose to follow the way,
it leads back to the path,
the path of divine service."
Openhand

Whatever our mission here is, it is likely that we will now get an authentic taste of it. Let us be absolutely clear though, in my experience, it is highly unlikely that we will be trusted with the full unfettered support and resources of Benevolent Consciousness to fulfil that mission yet. Why not? After Transfiguration it is highly likely, perhaps unavoidable, that a new shadow identity will arise. It happens as the newly transfigured being senses the divine purity of the reconnected soul flowing within; there is a tendency to want to own these heavenly essences. We may feel the presence of Christ or Buddha-like consciousness and think we are they. Or alternatively, we might struggle with the experience of non-identified presence and not be able to simply rest in pure beingness without questioning that state. It is as if fragments of the soul are still attaching to the bodymind in some way, thus creating a shadow identity.

So whilst the Transfiguration is a miraculous transition in our journey, it is still not the end of the story. Next, if we continue to follow the path, Benevolent Consciousness will help expose the shadow in us, so that it may be 'crucified' on the altar of unadulterated, absolute truth.

Gateway 4
"Enlightenment"

"Your pain is the breaking of the shell
that encloses your understanding.
Even as the stone of the fruit must break,
that its heart may stand in the sun,
so must you know your pain."
Kahlil Gibran

Key: confront karma

From the author's memoirs...

I was sat close to the front in the quaint Spiritualist Church listening intently to the Sunday evening medium helping people make connections with the dearly departed. Of course mediumship has been much criticised even ridiculed within society, but it seems to me this scepticism is mostly born of ignorance. I am convinced had any critic taken the time and conscience to visit such a humble, spiritual abode, neither with pretence nor need of justification, what they would have inescapably discovered was a profoundly beautiful and divinely loving approach to spirituality. I witnessed countless connections by mediums who could not possibly have known the details they revealed without some bridge to the 'other side'.

On this particular Sunday, the medium was a wizened old lady. Teetering on a walking stick she may have been, but her croaky voice only very thinly veiled a rock steady self acceptance. I had not seen her before, but it quickly became apparent that she had neither the need for people to accept her, nor her clairvoyant discernments. Through tired and wrinkled skin her light shone nevertheless very brightly. She was simply and awesomely okay to deliver exactly what she got with no frills, but with astounding self assurance and belief.

The evening was drawing to a close when suddenly she appeared to be receiving a communication. After a moment or two of quiet reflection, she looked up and without hesitation pointed her bony finger directly at me. "You Sir, I have a message to give you. Whilst you may look completely relaxed on the outside, on the inside is a hidden tension. You were involved in a car crash a few years back were you not?", "Yes" I replied rather meekly. She continued "Well you've been living on a life support machine ever since and your guides would like you to switch it off now. That's all I have to give you." I was completely taken a back. What on earth could she mean?

The next day found me at my desk lost in my own inner world quietly contemplating the curious exchange of the previous evening. When nothing immediately came to mind, I resorted to the approach I should have best begun with - asking the universe! So I went inwards, using breath to quieten the mind. I allowed the question to arise "What is the universe revealing to me now?" and felt it radiate outwards. It didn't take long to be answered - it never did. My attention was immediately drawn to a picture I had on the wall in the corner of the room. It was of the Oxford and Cambridge Varsity Boat Race. I had rowed in Isis, the reserve team, which in 1985 had beaten Cambridge in record time. At the time, it had been a proud achievement for me and the picture now adorned my wall hanging over the trophy cabinet containing many other medals, photos and achievements of the past.

It was suddenly clear where I had gone 'wrong'. In my divorce settlement, I had relinquished everything we jointly owned bar for a couple of pieces of furniture. Why then had I felt the need to keep the trophy cabinet? "Was there still an attachment to achievement?" I inwardly asked. At precisely that moment, all the electricity went off in the building! It seemed I had my answer. "Perhaps then the life support machine analogy meant that a little part of my ego was still clinging to life?" The lights suddenly sprang on again providing me an unmistakable answer. I was soon to be heading off to complete an Easter fast in Israel's Negev Desert, "Maybe then I should get rid of the trophy cabinet together with all the medals, awards and photos of my previous life before I go?" Once again all the lights went off in the building! The guidance was unequivocal.

So it was, that on the Thursday before Easter 2005, I had erected a huge bonfire upon which I was now busily bestowing any final reminder of my former life; I was signalling my purpose to smoke out and confront any attachment to identity which might still be lingering within. On top went my treasured Karate Black Belt; my Commando Green Beret; Gulf War medals earned during the liberation of Kuwait; various sporting trophies; my degree certificate along with a whole array of nostalgic photos. Finally on top, I placed the most meaningful accolade I still possessed - the rowing blade I used in the Boat Race still ingrained with the blood, sweat and tears the achievement had cost. As I carried the wooden blade across my shoulders towards the 'funeral pyre', tears began rolling down my cheeks. They were tears both of sadness at the sense of loss and also ones of deep joy. I recognised that finally, liberation was beckoning me. As I watched the dancing flames engulf the last vestiges of nostalgic memorabilia, I could not help feeling I was being guided to some final crucifixion. Painful as it may have been, I knew that courage would always be rewarded with some synchronistic recognition for effort by the ever watchful eye of Benevolent Consciousness. As I went to survey the ashes the next day, seemingly nothing had withstood the intense heat, even pewter had melted. Then floating around on the surface of the ashes, I noticed a pink card which had somehow miraculously survived the blaze. My attention was drawn to these four words: "degree ceremony, admit one". I was no longer in any doubt; I had received my invitation to step into Gateway 4.

It was now Easter Friday and in keeping with tradition (well sort of!) it all began with a 'last supper' of pizza and red wine in Cafe Uno at Heathrow International Airport. It all seems a bit cheesy now, but I was simply responding to an inner pull to act reinforced by the synchronistic confirmations of Benevolent Consciousness. I was departing for a twenty one day fast in Israel's Negev Desert seemingly to break through the mental identification - the "shadow" - that was dimming the light of my soul and preventing the Enlightenment of the non-identified Seer shining through my being.

Having spent Easter itself in Jerusalem, my drop off point in the Negev was at one end of the Ramon Crater approximately 30 miles from the border with Egypt and the Sinai. The Ramon Crater is an outstanding natural beauty, a sort of miniature version of the Grand Canyon. Although quite rocky and arid, it still had patches of vegetation with early spring flowers. A seasonal blip meant it was a lot hotter than I had been led to expect, so I hiked mostly in darkness and rested during the day.

Late one evening, having reached the far edge of the crater, only a few miles from the inviting quietness of the Sinai, I stopped to lie down and rest. Finding myself a degree of comfort in a shallow ditch by the side of the central track, I looked up at the twinkling stars in the dark night sky and began to release inner tightness and efforting within my bodymind. Hunger had long since subsided and the quieter inner metabolism meant that my consciousness could easily expand, thus intensifying the connection with universal life energy. Finally, I felt myself beginning to dissolve into infinite oneness. I knew my awareness was right on the very tip of non-identified experience, dissociated completely even from the interconnectedness of Unity Consciousness. I was teetering on the verge of the absoluteness I'd tasted briefly at Transfiguration - the non-identified Seer of all things.

Then right at that very moment where I was finally poised delicately on the edge of the void, my attention was drawn to distant footsteps making their way along the track in the direction of where I lay. As the sound drew closer, it was clear there was more than one person and then suddenly it dawned, this was a group of people marching in time together - an Israeli platoon no less! What would they make of this strange bearded foreigner dressed in desert style ex military clothing lying covertly in a ditch in the middle of their desert? The prospect of a few weeks interrogation at the hands of Mossad did not seem a very inviting prospect. Not at all what I had intended. Yet again my consciousness was brought to the hidden dangers of intention and expectation!

I had no choice but to surrender to the flow of events and lay quietly whilst the universe rolled the dice. Perhaps Higher Guidance was playing a game of "chicken" with me. Fortunately, it was not my destiny to be discovered. Although only a few feet away, the platoon marched right past me without noticing a thing. As they disappeared into the distance, I began to chuckle, then cackle and finally burst into raucous laughter. Yes, the universe was having an immense cosmic joke at my expense!

My fast ended prematurely precisely at that moment - I no longer needed to achieve anything. I should shut up, pack up and go home which is exactly what I intended to do. But if I have learned one thing in my spiritual life, it is that Benevolent Consciousness likes to catch us unaware. Just when we think we have got the lesson we came for, just when we are completely off guard, that is when our benevolent guiding hand likes to strike. What surprise would it be if we had an inkling of what was going to happen next? How can you expose an imposter if it knows exactly what is about to happen? No, to truly smoke out the shadow, we have to be caught completely unaware.

I decided I would end my expedition early and make my way back home. Although by now I was getting quite tired, I felt to take in some of the natural beauty spots I had passed along the way. Making my way back along the Ramon Crater, my attention was drawn to a weather beaten sign pointing to the "Prism Gorge". I felt a clear inner pull to take a look, but did not question too much the curious sounding name - why had they used the name "Prism"? It failed to occur to me at the time that a prism breaks down light into its component parts - another way of putting it might be "bringing into the light that which is normally hidden from view". Sometimes synchronicity works that way - we only know what the 'omens' mean after the event has transpired!

The Prism Gorge had many outstanding natural qualities and very quickly I was lost in its captivating beauty not noticing how the bare rock surfaces harnessed and intensified the sun's heat. By the time I felt the magnifying effect of its burning rays, it was too late to retrace my steps, I would need to find shelter. But there was no shelter! Clearly that is why they named it after a prism which captures and intensifies light - it certainly did not shade it. So I erected a bivouac between two rocks to provide a little shade under which to hide.

The heat of the sun grew stronger and stronger seemingly

catching me in direct line no matter how I wriggled and shuffled. Within a few hours of seemingly intense heat, I felt dehydrated and sun stricken. After a couple more hours I was becoming delirious and hallucinating. Unable any longer to move my weather beaten body, it seemed as if it was time to expire completely. Visions of memorable bygone events drifted in and out of my awareness. All those times where I had efforted and struggled to achieve, where I had craved peer acceptance to fulfil lack of self esteem. The final most testing experience to appear was the Royal Marine Commando Course. Synchronistically, I was carrying with me the little red dagger arm patch that marines wear on their uniform. I always carried it to remind me to keep going in times of difficulty. As I took it out of my pocket, I noticed that upside down it reminded me of a crucifix - a burning red cross - this indeed was a crucifixion of my ego. At that point it did not matter to me any longer whether I lived or died. I had seen my shadow, the imposter of achievement, glamour and efforting masquerading in a world of selfless, spiritual service. I buried the dagger to signify my readiness to 'bury' my shadow and surrendered to the seemingly inevitable, at which point there was once more the sublime taste of the tasteless - the unidentified Seer - before I drifted off to a placeless place.

Initially I was not exactly sure whether I was still alive or dead (at least in a physical sense), but after an unknown period of time, somehow an angelic energy lifted me onto my feet and carried me forwards. It took me two further days and nights to stagger out of the crater. Having long since lost my bearings, I no longer either knew nor really cared whether I would make it back or not. Then suddenly, as if out of nowhere, I stumbled into an encampment. Of all the things it might have been, it turned out to be a retreat centre! At the entrance was an attractive, Middle-Eastern lady with long dark hair sitting in the shade reading a book. She carried a strong Magdalene energy. Introducing herself as "Noah" and greeting me with a warm smile... "Yes we have one bed left" she offered, without me even opening my lips. There was no longer any doubt; I had died and gone to heaven!

Gateway 4
-overview-

By now on our journey, we will have made the crucial switch from identifying ourselves as the false self to becoming the Seer expressed as the soul through the bodymind. In other words, we experience ourselves (perhaps for the first time) as non-identified presence, what some might call "God". It is a simple state of pure clarity existing in the background of all activity. It is so ordinary, so normal and yet so miraculous, that when we finally dissolve into it, we may feel like every light in the universe has just been switched on simultaneously.

Yet when we are looking for it, or when we cannot accept it as the target of all our searching, efforting and longing, then suddenly we become separated from it once more. How can you see yourself when you are all there is? Here is the divine paradox then - when we are looking for it, it remains always just out of reach like a young child grasping at a helium filled balloon; but when we just let go and open ourselves up, the 'target' of our aspiration moves to us. In other words, we fall into it.

It is metaphored wonderfully for us in the place of all clear answers - Mother Nature. Consider the Kingfisher; since light refracts (bends) when it leaves the surface of water, the Kingfisher never actually sees the exact location of the fish. It simply heads for the image but knows at some point, that it must step off its trajectory and delve completely into the unknown. Ignoring the image itself - the illusionary reality - it dives through the surface into absolute truth, whereupon its goal is finally realised.

So it is with the soul. The soul is our trajectory to an illusionary target. We follow the path, but at some point, we will see past the target and simply fall into the truth. Then we become the truth and have continual experiences of it; all of life offers the opportunity to taste the constant crystal clear clarity of non-identified presence. Thoughts, emotions, feelings and even the heartfelt longing of the soul all arise within this infinite, unadulterated potential and yet it remains always there - the Seer - an inviolable eternal existence.

At this point we are in an enlightened state, flowing freely without self identification and without attachment to the drama of life. It is in such a state that we - as the Seer - feel the soul for the first time in all its purity. It arises within us and flows through the various layers of the bodymind. Whilst we may not grasp it in our minds (because there is no need to) we can still intrinsically recognise the characteristics of our soul as an harmonic of different essences, what I refer to as the "Seven Rays of Divine Impulse". My personal experiences of these are as follows...

Ray 7: shaping co-creative magic
Ray 7 provides the magical impact of the soul in our life's journey. If we are able to master our inner distortions and pause just long enough in the drama of life, then we will allow in spontaneous, synchronistic and co-creative magic to change the surrounding field for the maximum benefit and upliftment of all. In this way, Ray 7 inspires life's true magicians.

Ray 6: realising authentic self expression
Ray 6 inspires us stay continually focussed on our life's purpose - to realise, unfold and express who we really are. It generates commitment and devotion to our cause; to glorify our soul in all its brilliant colour. It is that unquenchable driving force to express our innate qualities and inspire others to shine their inner light too. Humanity's philosophers, spiritual leaders and artists are all greatly driven by the Ray 6 influence.

Ray 5: manifesting unique possibility

All souls are connected and when expressing authentically are completely aligned with the divine flow. And yet each is divinely configured to deliver a unique pathway in the river of life. The complete story of the One Life is generated by the collation of many individual chapters. So the Ray 5 writes for each of us our unique destiny, that which allows the fullest expression of our individuality. The Ray 5 animates life's entrepreneurs.

Ray 4: harmonising through right resolution

Ray 4 is the divine rationalising energy which helps us find right resolution with our environment and other sentient life. It is the ray impulse which blends passion with compassion. It provides the discernment to confront unjust situations in a non judgmental way. Its purpose is to break apart the lower harmony to find a more equitable higher one. People with highly active Ray 4 tend to be life's diplomats, politicians and teachers. To me, Ray 4 is the "Christ Consciousness."

Ray 3: interpreting absolute authentic reality

Ray 3 harnesses and processes higher abstract wisdom delivering it in a form that can provide a clear interpretation of our current, absolute authentic reality. In other words, it's how we know what's really real. People with strong Ray 3 influence are the scientists and translators of life able to dissect and deliver abstract wisdom bringing the formless into form in such a way that can be understood and utilised by many.

Ray 2: surrendering divine openness

This is the powerful, self sacrificing influence of unconditional love for all life. It represents the divinely feminine principle of surrendered openness throughout the universe; the harmonising impetus willingly embracing and not judging the inherent imperfection of all creations and situations. Ray 2 holds the infinite wisdom and knowledge of life.

Ray 1: focussing divine purpose
This is the driving inner sense of purpose to create. It is the manifestation of the divine masculine principle throughout the universe. From the place of separation, it is that undeniable inner resolve to find a higher level of unity and oneness both within ourselves and between all sentient beings. It causes us to challenge and break apart the status quo which may be holding us in a lower level of understanding and clarity.

Despite the blissful experiences of the soul coursing through the bodymind, it is not yet fully unleashed in its entirety. In other words, the soul is not yet fully reconnected and integral within our being. Why not? It is at the point where we really begin to experience this deep soul infusion that the shadow identity arises. This is where the soul becomes attached to previous circumstances in past lives. As the soul flows through the causal body where such "karma" is stored, it is possible that a 'fragment' of the soul may get stuck, usually because we are still uncomfortable with a previous experience in some way and allow ourselves to become identified with it. It is this fragment of the soul which forms the shadow acting as a surreptitious imposter tainting our authentic impulses.

Another way of looking at it, is that under particular circumstances and conditions, we are unable to hold our centre of non-identified presence and still require some form of internal reference to hang on to. We are not yet completely free to be the Seer and to let go in all circumstances. It is then that as the shadow, we may become identified with the profound beauty of the soul. It is typical, for example, that people describe what they may experience as a powerful Christ-like or Buddha presence within them. These are harmonics of the seven rays and their essences are so pure, so miraculous and so well known, that we may seek to 'own' them within. In other words there is a fragment of ourselves trying to 'model' us into something it considers it should be. In some ways then, the shadow becomes an 'echo' of the soul.

This shadow identity is much more subtle than previously experienced. Unlike its predecessors (such as the inner child and inner teenager), impulses to act are not initiated within it, they always come from the soul, however by acting as a filter, the shadow can distort or dim the divine light of the soul. So typically for example, we may be engaged in spiritual, apparently selfless work of some kind, but the presence of the shadow may ensure there is always a form of pay back for the personality in the shape of some material, emotional or egotistical gain. So whilst we may have begun serving humanity as an apparently selfless lightworker, there may be a hidden, unspoken and delicately subtle individual motivation. So subtle is this identity, that we even have difficulty seeing it ourselves. It may manifest for example as the slightest trace of efforting to reach many people, heal the sick, save the planet, protect Mother Nature etc. It could be that the soul is authentically given to do these things, but ownership of that purpose will add that extra bit of energy, the extra impetus that over-eggs perfect delivery of Right Action.

It is exactly this obscuring energy which ultimately turns away those people of the correct vibration to receive our particular transmission. It could be that we still reach many people and that a message is transmitted, however, is it exactly the right message for exactly the right people? So it is this internal shadow identity that we must deal with during the Gateway 4 transition.

The key to dissolving the shadow is to understand where it comes from and how it operates. As previously stated, the shadow forms when the light of the soul gets 'stuck on something'. So the soul touches past life karma as it flows through the causal body and activates it. In other words, this layer of consciousness begins to influence many patterns of experience in our lives. Events are manifested to create external 'images', that we may see and better understand the blockages we are activating. We are now being given the opportunity to confront and deal with our past life karma.

The key to processing and releasing the karma thereby dissolving the shadow, is to identify which distortions are arising. So it helps to know which forms the shadow can arise in. Here are some typical ones I have experienced...

- **the false profit:** owning the selfless actions of the soul requiring a 'payback' thus rendering selfless actions less effective
- **the controller:** not fully trusting in the natural flow of the universe, thereby subtly needing to control events
- **the questioner:** continually questioning the authentic impulses of the soul or the experience of non-identified presence
- **the dissolver:** wanting to protect the state of non identification therefore dissolving the soul's impulse
- **the restrainer:** restraining a spontaneous impulse of passionate action thereby dulling its full impact
- **the distorter:** distorting an authentic action causing uncertainty and therefore loss of effectiveness
- **the absolutist:** needing to always express absolute truth, whatever the cost, thereby unnecessarily damaging the energetic harmony of the moment.

It is also important to realise that the shadow serves an important beneficial function too. By owning the natural impulses of the soul as they arise through our personality, the shadow ensures that the impulses gain traction in the dense energetic environment of the bodymind. It could be the case that without this additional support, the impulses might dissolve just as soon as they arise - that is until the newly transfigured being becomes adept at feeling and attuning to the arising impulses and acting on them, even though they might be quite gentle.

So the presence of the shadow is a double edged sword with both important benefits and drawbacks. In the beginning, we benefit from amplified expression of our higher knowing; however, just as a growing child is nurtured and protected by its parents, it must at some point be weaned off this support if it is to stand wholly and squarely on its own two feet. Likewise we must ultimately dissolve all shadow identities if we are to experience our ultimate destiny - the constant experience of non-identified presence. In other words Enlightenment.

There is another reason why the shadow cannot be allowed to persist within our consciousness. The fact that there is still some personal pay back required as a result of the shadow's presence (in whatever guise that might be), means that we are still susceptible to the temptations of Opposing Consciousness. In our evolved state, it is likely that we can be highly influential to others embarked on their own spiritual path. Thus if the messages being infused downwards from the Source are being subtly distorted, then there is increasing potential for more and more people to be led astray. Hence it is not until we have dissolved all shadow identities that we can be fully trusted by Benevolent Consciousness to help unfold the Divine Purpose. That is why (in my view) authentic spiritual work is only provided resources gradually. Rapid success on the other hand, can tend to indicate the distorting influence of Opposing Consciousness leading people off track.

This is an extremely difficult predicament. On our journey to this point, we will have learned the importance of listening to our own inner voice as opposed to being overly influenced by others. We will have become adept at distinguishing where impulses are genuinely from the soul and where they are not and since we are now always flowing as the soul, we know the origination of the impulse is always authentic. We also become aware of the importance of spontaneity and so increasingly, we simply allow our expression to flow. We tend to process our actions less and instead continually settle into pure presence; we realise the very act of processing what we are being can take us out of our experience of the Seer. So as the soul arises out of the stillness, the shadow is cast, but as soon as we settle again, the shadow disappears!

It is at this point that only dramatic action can really expose the shadow. It comes in the form of what some have called the "crucifixion". We must catch the shadow unaware and notice the effects of its influence even after it has disappeared from view. At this point, if we allow it to, Benevolent Consciousness will guide us to events to expose the effects of our shadow; where we are being less than selfless, where we are in fear of something, where we need success, or are lacking ultimate trust in the universe. We are then caused to feel the full pain of the shadow's attachment - our karma - so that instead we may continually realign to our centre, the place of non-identified presence, in which case the shadow will dissolve.

This could possibly happen during one powerful event as I have described in my own personal experience in the Negev. However, it is more likely to happen over a protracted period of time, especially if we have several shadow identities to dissolve, which is mostly the case. In this way, we are caused to sacrifice ourselves on the final altar of absolute truth. We are guided on a seemingly self destructive path so that the wheat can be separated from the chaff. Extreme circumstances are created to 'rattle our cage' so that suddenly it becomes abundantly clear where we have been getting stuck. Moments such as these indicate clearly that we are now truly transitioning the fourth corridor. The hidden fears, desires or ambitions of the shadow - the manifestations of our karma - are exposed and brought into the light.

If we keep surrendering in the jaws of fear and doubt, in other words if we keep having the courage to let go, despite whatever may be happening for us, then the fragments of the soul lost within the causal body begin to reintegrate. Whilst we may have previously gained insight into some past life influences, it is here that the full, shocking recognition of what we have been through finally dawns.

We may experience incredible visions of ageless experiences that have shaped our souls from the very dawning of time itself. Many of these will be tainted with fear and suffering as the emergent soul has been unfolding itself to ever increasing sophistication and understanding...

> *"Suffering is generated where there is lack*
> *of understanding as to the absolute order of things.*
> *It is merely a mirror by which to see the soul,*
> *something so pure, so radiant, so spectacular,*
> *that when it unfolds into its full brilliance,*
> *even suffering can no longer be regarded as such."*
> Openhand

Our karmic attachments are the final constraint limiting the soul from full unbridled reintegration within our being. If we have the courage to confront the shadow identities by following the path laid before us, then ultimately we will find ourselves bathing in the pain of all our distortions - all our final self deceptions. Here is the ultimate test; we are entering the inner sanctum of God, but are being asked to crawl unceremoniously to the altar. We delve deeply into our distortions and with the flail of profound self honesty, we are laid bare. The shadow is exposed before us and is enveloped by a tidal wave of light.

In that moment, we are washed through with the full consciousness of humanity, Mother Earth and our planetary system. The causal body has been purified thereby dissolving the final restraint limiting us from the unadulterated, ultimate joy of harmonious unity. It is a bitter sweet experience. It simultaneously exposes us to the awesome majesty of being and the all pervading suffering of universal Separation Consciousness.

Temporarily, we may be overwhelmed by the experience and get sucked into the internal/external drama once more, but fairly quickly, the soul - an expression of the Seer - normalises in this new unprotected, unsheathed environment. The tsunami has passed, the ship rights itself and we quickly attune to the new way of being.

Now we have tasted consciously the full pain and suffering of separation from God. We have not shirked, but drank it in through every pore. We have submerged ourselves, willingly drowned and discovered the true essence we were seeking all along - that which cannot be violated even in the midst of absolute violation. We have transcended the inner fires of hell, burned away the dross of the shadow and yielded to the sublime taste of absoluteness through all things. Finally, we dissolve into Enlightenment. The Fourth Gateway has been transcended.

Transitioning Gateway 4
-useful tools-

1. Self vigilance: *watch for the presence of the shadow, where we might be acting from a less than authentic, selfless purpose.*
2. Follow genuine guidance: *identify the negative influence of Opposing Consciousness. Follow genuine guidance at whatever apparent personal cost.*
3. Confront karma and release attachment: *confront, process and release attachment to past life karma as our consciousness expands into the causal body.*
4. Find the key to surrender: *surrender absolutely into our karmic regressions and the key to the inner sanctum will appear.*
5. Enlightenment: *settle into complete self acceptance and assume rightful inner perception of the fully enlightened being.*

1. Self vigilance: *watch for the presence of the shadow, where we might be acting from a less than authentic, selfless purpose.*

The shadow identity is unlike any filter we have previously encountered (such as the inner child or teenager). As we transition from identification with the bodymind to experiencing ourselves as the soul (in other words as Transfiguration happens), there is still a tendency for fragments of the soul to identify with the bodymind, perhaps because we are as yet uncomfortable with the experience of non-identified presence. Consequently a shadow identity forms.

This filter is extremely difficult to notice because we feel whole, genuine and complete. It is a very powerful self deception, the shadow knows that there is no need to be attached to anything; it knows that we can trust absolutely in the benevolence of the universe; it knows that we cannot die; it knows that the soul gives selfless service; it knows that we are at one with all creation. This is exactly the problem - there is an identity knowing these qualities rather than just being present with them. In other words, the shadow begins to subtly own them.

To 'smoke out' the imposter (assuming we are ready to do that) we must apply extra self vigilance. It is likely that by now we will be consciously involved in spiritual work of one form or another - perhaps helping others to unfold. As the unadulterated soul, there is no need of pay back for what we do and yet at the same time, the soul will always be a custodian of Right Action. In other words, it is bound to ensure there is correct energetic exchange in all actions. So the soul will seek to ensure that the correct balance is achieved; energy is given out in one form and received in another. For example, in my view, it is entirely correct that we be paid for spiritual work and this would always be felt as the Right Action of the universe harmonising and balancing itself out. Were this not the case, the soul might not be able to summon the correct amount of physical energy (in the form of money for example) for its work to continue.

So if we keep watching ourselves we may notice a slight attachment to receiving payment for example. Another distortion to watch for is glamour. It may be that we are destined to have a high profile and it might be entirely appropriate to exhibit a strong personality in order that more people can be reached. Such a strong energy can easily be distorted and thereby limit our effectiveness in carrying out our work - others may sense the presence of non-selfless ego for example.

The shadow could appear in many other guises. For instance, whilst we feel a strong authentic pull to help others, we may get attached to their suffering; or we may notice that we frequently hold the keys to another's unfolding and then get attached to whether they accept the keys or not. All are clear signs of where our shadow is active. In which case, the important thing is to be vigilant about our motivations for doing things. Do our actions serve the purpose of the whole? Or is a part of us secretly revelling in the attention? If the latter is the case, we can be sure we have spotted our shadow.

A good barometer is to continually assess our level of internal peace. Do we notice a very subtle inner efforting different from the natural arising of authentic purpose? Self honesty at this point is vital if we are to expose and dissolve the shadow.

2. Follow genuine guidance: *identify the negative influence of Opposing Consciousness. Follow genuine guidance at whatever apparent personal cost.*
By now we may have realised that there are two types of consciousness at work within the surrounding energy field influencing our unfolding. Benevolent Consciousness has our highest interests at heart. It will speak to us through synchronicity. It helps by providing a mirror, amplifying an inner pull to act and will guide us to Right Action where everything seems to click magically into place or it will guide us to challenges to expose the shadow.

The agenda of Opposing Consciousness on the other hand is to retard our spiritual evolution. It does so by 'feeding the shadow'. In other words, it has the ability to manifest outcomes which serve the shadow, amplifying and building its identity within. I have noticed through many examples that it will build either on our hidden fears or desires. We may find for instance that a clear pathway rapidly unfolds before us whereby we are able to reach many people, but the distortion of our delivery may be less than authentic. We either exaggerate the message or dilute it. In either case, if we are not careful, our transmission can lead people astray.

Initially it can be extremely difficult to know that the help we are receiving is not from the purest source - especially because the shadow will feel very good about its new found abundance. It is possible we have already expected this sort of manifestation as a result of our increasing at-one-ment with the creative power of the universe. The key is to watch for any subtle efforting; whereas our energies were previously rising, now they are being restricted. This is a sure sign that we are 'leaking' emotional energy through our shadow. It is this that Opposing Consciousness farms us for. If we are not careful, we build a whole new false lifestyle to feed our growing shadow identity.

This is where Benevolent Consciousness will lend a hand if we are prepared to follow it. We may find that guidance seems to pull in two different directions. Authentic guidance tends to be more sophisticated and spontaneous, where synchronicity supports direct inner knowing imparted through the higher chakras. The guidance of Opposing Consciousness on the other hand, is a little more 'clunky'. It is less spontaneous, tends to work at the level of the lower mind and is less able to influence deep inner yearnings. So when we watch synchronicity apparently guiding us forwards, it always pays to check how we really feel about the options. If synchronicity is in line with our inner knowing or a deep heartfelt pull, then the guidance is likely to be genuine.

3. Confront karma and release attachment: *confront, process and release attachment to past life karma as our consciousness expands into the causal body.*

As our consciousness continues to expand, we unfold into the causal body. This process activates past life regressions, recreating essences of the previous incarnations through the patterns of our current lives. Frequently, this mirror may be supported by visions, inner knowing and most importantly as pain or tightness in the bodymind. It could be that a pain or injury suddenly appears when there has been no apparent cause. Or we may suddenly feel ourselves becoming 'toxic' as the negative energy washes through our system. It may even be that we hold a long standing physical or emotional condition caused by our karma. The combination of all of these things can be deeply unsettling and destabilising.

If we bring our attention to the problem, then this tightness will manifest synchronistically through circumstances in our lives. In other words, events shape to mirror back the original experience in a past life which the shadow is attached to; the essence of our suffering caused by the trauma of the original incident is recreated. If we can continue through the current event, watch ourselves in the suffering and surrender into it, then Right Action will become clear to us and by following this instead of the conditioned behaviour arising from the attachment, then we can identify and release the karma by fully bathing ourselves in it.

For example, it may be that we hold a grudge against someone for not supporting and helping us - it may be that in the past life they seriously let us down, resulting in injury or death. Now a new relationship materialises where we are once more invited to notice our lack of trust in a situation of great importance. It may stir up all kinds of resentment, frustration, disappointment and anger. Perhaps this time, if guided to do so, we can seize the opportunity to 'go out on a limb' and trust once more. In my experience, processes such as these will continue until we have confronted all our karma.

4. Find the key to surrender: *surrender absolutely into our karmic regressions and the key to the inner sanctum will appear.*
When we have summoned the courage to confront our karma, we will at times be brought to the threshold of our physical, mental and emotional endurance and then at crucial moments, be invited to dive through that threshold. It may feel we are being brought to the very limits of sanity; we are being invited to destroy all remaining attachment to individual self identification.

It is in these moments where the pain and suffering may seem almost unbearable, that we must watch for an alternative experience within. If we keep observing, we will find a key that opens the doorway once more into non-identified presence, which is always there, even amidst the depths of suffering. From that serene place, we can taste even the fullness of the negative energy washing over us and yet not be lost in it.

The key itself may be something as simple as a word such as "openness", "transparency" or "liberation". It may be a vision or a symbol or it could be a particular exercise. Whatever it is, we will each have a key and it has the power to unlock the doorway for us into that sublime, non-identified state.

When we have released our attachment in this way and found our way back to the inner sanctum by the appropriate use of our key, we may also dissolve away any negative energy that has now been unleashed through our system. This may be achieved using "deep consciousness body work" of some kind. In other words, a practice that brings our attention into the deepest recesses of our physical body and flushes it through with 'clean' energy. So for example, it could be practices such as Yoga, Tai Chi, the Martial Arts and dance etc. It could even be energetic walking. There are some specifically designed processes such as "Tibetan Pulsing", "Rolfing" and indeed our own "Openhand Meditation in Movement". It may be that a brisk walk in nature works for you. It could be Reiki or massage performed by someone else. Whatever it is, it will work most effectively when our attention is directed to deep inner layers of consciousness. We are being invited to let go, so that higher, purer energies may once again flood into our being.

Although extremely rigorous and testing, as with all Gateways, the only way out is through. At some point we surrender all and the courage materialises to carry us forward. At this point, the Gateway opens, not through efforting, but instead through total inner release.

5. Enlightenment: *settle into complete self acceptance and assume rightful inner perception of the fully enlightened being.*
During the Gateway 4 transition, our karma will be activated as either one or a range of shadow identities. Over time, each of these will be exposed and dissolved. If the transition turns out to be a protracted one, then we are likely to experience many 'descents into darkness' followed by corresponding re-emergences into the light. As all aspects of the shadow are dissolved, we - as the soul - are finally liberated and become fully enlightened within our being. The soul is no longer fragmented, it no longer gets stuck within the bodymind and we remain in the state of non-identified presence no matter what is happening to us. Our 'mission' to remember ourselves as what we really are has been accomplished.

The experience of this is unique for each of us. It has been described as a sense of "rising", "total expansion", "crystal clear clarity" or an "awesome state of pure presence". Whatever happens for us, it will be abundantly clear this final shift has taken place. It will help at this point to simply settle into that state and allow it to flood our experience.

As before, passing through the Enlightenment Gateway will be marked by some external ceremony or other - something which is deeply recognisable and remains forever etched into our cellular memory. We are now a fully enlightened being.

Transitioning Gateway 4
-general misconceptions-

1. That we are being completely authentic

At Transfiguration, there is a major shift of inner perception to experiencing ourselves as the soul through the bodymind. Whilst we may have moved to the place of inner authenticity, there may still be fragments of the soul identifying with the external drama and needing something to happen. Consequently, a shadow will form, which is so closely aligned with authentic purpose (the genuine pull of the soul), that it is exceedingly difficult for us to see the distortion. We feel we are acting with complete authenticity and it is very hard for anyone to convince us otherwise. This is where we must continue to surrender to benevolent higher guidance, to bring us to situations that expose and dissolve the shadow.

2. That all guidance is right guidance

It is likely that by this stage in our evolution, we will be very adept at reading synchronicity and thereby understanding what we are being guided to do. However, all guidance is not benevolent and whilst we have an inner shadow, it is still quite easy to be deceived. So for example, synchronicity can be manipulated and our inner pull distorted to throw us off our pathway. Consequently, at this stage, it is of utmost importance that we become completely familiar with the vibration of our inner pull and watch where it might not be so genuine. Maybe for example, a flow of internal energy causes a negative imbalance, loss of peace and harmony. It is of great importance to be doubly sure about the guidance we are receiving before we act. Hence we must always measure an inner pull against external synchronicity. One form of guidance will give us the feeling of being completely at one with the universe, the other will always leave us feeling slightly at odds internally.

3. That our manifestations are correct and fully supported

The more we follow the Right Action of the universe, the more we witness acts of synchronistic and co-creative magic. Eventually, we settle into the knowing that all manifestations are created by consciousness. We cease being lured into the illusion of trying to shape the external drama. Instead, we look for what we believe should happen in accordance with the correct flow of energy. The problem we may encounter, is that of Opposing Consciousness throwing us off the correct pathway. It does this by distorting the downward flow of our soul through negative interference in the lower chakras. Opposing Consciousness has the ability to manifest in support of a subtle hidden desire. In supporting our action, it may deceive us into thinking we are correctly aligned with the authentic purpose of our soul. It is easy to be duped when we first achieve apparent success. From experience therefore, we are unlikely to receive the full resource support of Benevolent Consciousness until we have dissolved all shadows and transitioned Gateway 4.

4. That Enlightenment means losing personality

Although we are being invited to humble ourselves and open up to inner scrutiny, it does not mean that we need to somehow dissolve the personality in order to be enlightened. If there was an identity within trying to do this, then we have once more created separation, thereby removing us from the experience of non-identified presence. When there is no identity limiting the soul, the authentic energy of purpose will flow unhindered through our bodymind, animating as the personality, our divine expression of the soul.

Sometimes that personality can be quiet, peaceful and retiring. At other times it might appear energetic, purposeful and animated with charisma. It all depends on the natural flow of the universe, how the soul aligns with it and how that energy is transmitted through the bodily vehicles of expression. Each soul is unique and expresses itself in unique ways according to the 'lay of the land' and the requirements of the moment.

5. In Enlightenment all pain, illness and disease disappear
There is sometimes the misconception that in Enlightenment all pain, illness and disease disappear. Indeed this goal is often held up as something to which we should aspire. In my experience however, in Enlightenment, we are not acting from a phenomenal centre at all - we are simply not a person. As such, in non-identifed presence, there is simply no attachment to good health and ease. If we are efforting to cure ourselves, we have certainly once more created a separate identity and another barrier between us and completeness. In Enlightenment, we feel our interconnectedness to the extent that we know someone else's dis-ease by feeling it within our own selves. We know that the dis-ease will be removed as and when it is meant to. We do not identify with the problem at all; we are simply flowing with Right Action and if that means it is right for us to have a particular experience, even illness, there is no turning away from it. There is only absolute, unconditional self acceptance. In my experience of Enlightenment, the pain does not get less, it may even get worse, it just matters less!

Transitioning Gateway 4
-signs of beginning-

At the Transfiguration (Gateway 3), we will have tasted the wonderful liberation of pure, non-identified presence perhaps for the first time. Soon after that, if not immediately, the inner shadow will have emerged to own that sublime state of perception and so it distorts and dims the true brilliance of our unfettered, inner light. For a while, this may not seem to matter, because we will still be channelling powerful energies from the Source and are probably beginning to be quite successful in our spiritual work. It could be we are convinced that we have already reached Enlightenment.

In this situation, there is the risk that the shadow identity may become embedded in our state of perception. Perhaps that is why at this point in our evolution, Benevolent Consciousness seems to work particularly hard in causing us to confront this distortion. So it is likely we will feel the pull to encounter powerfully emotive circumstances; events to question us right to the very core of our being. When this starts to happen, we can be sure we have stepped into Gateway 4.

When the Gateway 4 transition to Enlightenment commences in earnest, it may seem like we have been wrong footed by Benevolent Consciousness and tested to the very limit of our endurance either physically, emotionally or mentally. It is in the final moment, where the shadow is still clinging on, that we may be caused to see the futility of struggle; to confront that subtle inner efforting and completely let go, whatever the cost might be. So although we cannot fully prepare for this "crucifixion", by knowing some of the pointers, we will be more able to recognise it taking place and therefore more able to surrender completely.

Here then are some of the pointers to Gateway 4...

- *we become increasingly familiar with the characteristics of our soul and its blend of different influences;*
- *we may experience a rapidly growing overtness and projection of spiritual activity accompanied by rapid material or spiritual 'success' (when supported by Opposing Consciousness);*
- *we will likely be sensing increasing help from higher realms (although sometimes misguided by Opposing Consciousness);*
- *a sudden realisation of apparently diverging pathways and the knowing that genuinely guided action may lead to apparently quite severe personal cost;*
- *a sequence of core splitting events to take us to the very limit of our threshold and beyond.*

Transitioning Gateway 4
-signs of completion-

Completion of Gateway 4 is the ultimate paradox. On the one hand, we may have been through quite dramatic circumstances in order to dissolve the shadows and yet on the other hand, the final settling into Enlightenment is an awesomely ordinary state (in my experience at least). Unlike the other transitions, there is just the quiet, inner recognition that something has irrevocably changed. Although there will undoubtedly be a sense of accomplishment and a marked ceremony, there is no longer anyone 'in here' to own that state. There is simply no one to justify it, defend it or even support it. There is just pure, unadulterated beingness with no fireworks, major celebrations or unnecessary drama. No blissfulness, no travelling to 'far away' astral planes; it comes with no sense of pride or need for justification. It just simply 'is'.

So the moments of crystal clear clarity - beingness with no small 'I' - join up into one all-encompassing, spaceless and timeless experience. The soul arises from the centre of this experience as a clear 'knowing' or 'pull' to act, but no-one inside either denies the impetus or owns it. Words arise with no thought to pre-empt them; spontaneous, authentic action just happens. This then, is the full experience of Enlightenment (as I know it) and when we have reached it, there is no mistaking it.

Although at this point, anyone who is enlightened will probably not need to be told they are, it might benefit those who are not yet there to have an indication of what it is like. At the very least, it may cause those who still labour with the presence of an inner shadow, to notice that they are not being absolutely, one hundred per cent authentic.

Here then are some indicators of the completion of Gateway 4...

- the final release of past life karma;
- as the 'waters of the causal body break', a sudden expansion of consciousness leading to non-identified experience of both light and dark;
- the final recognition and release of our separation from the experience of the Seer - the Absolute;
- total liberation and flow of the soul within our being;
- resting continually in the state of non-localised, unidentified presence whatever events are taking place;
- whilst we as the Seer are non-identified and non separate from the all that is, we are still completely accepting and comfortable with the apparent duality of an individual soul;
- the sense of final accomplishment;
- action, including thoughts and words, seems to just arise without anything pre-empting them.

Gateway 4
-summary-

To me, Enlightenment is a heavenly paradox. We have lived perhaps countless lifetimes engaged in the external drama. We have laughed, cried, loved and lied, searched endlessly through the universe of separation seeking solutions for our longing. We have failed to realise all this time, that our searching simply creates a greater landscape through which to search. Having reached a goal, we have instantly created what the goal is not and in so doing created another chapter in our repetitive story.

At some point however, we tire of the efforting and may get a fleeting glimpse of the truth... the answer is not 'out there' at all, but 'in here'. So begins the next chapter in the story; "What is it that's in here? Who am I? What am I?" We will encounter a new list of questions and conundrums through the inner universe which we discover is just as large as the outer one! We may learn how to heal, how to leave the body, transcend multiple plains of existence, travel on astral plains, live on light, even walk on water, but if we are still searching, we are guaranteed not to have found our destination.

Then one day, perhaps an ordinary day just like any other, something truly profound happens. No, we have not just cured someone's cancer or brought another back from the dead, instead we have settled into an awesomely ordinary state of perception - pure presence, no questions arising and no need of answers. The great cosmic joke we have been playing on ourselves is that the sublime state of being was there in our awareness all the time. It never went away, it just got clouded by everything else. Just like the proverbial monkey first confronting a mirror, we became so engaged in our own reflection we simply forgot just to be the monkey...

"Where is the True Self?
I look deep within... it is not the body,
deeper still... it is not the mind... deeper and deeper,
until I find it is not even the part doing the looking.
Then finally the True Self reveals itself
in the deepest part of myself
and expands out of me to fill the universe
then in each moment I learn to become it,
that which is both looking and being looked upon
that which is both hearing and being heard
that which is both feeling and being felt
the search is over, the True Self that I looked for
was there all the time."
Openhand

So awesome is that state, so profoundly clear, so sublime, so without identity or separation that something within wants to own it. Enlightenment is not something to be attained, it is found by relinquishing all need to attain anything. So as soon as it arises, the tendency is for a shadow identity to form and own it again. This shadow is a deceptive animal. Just as soon as we recognise everything is not quite as clear as it once was, we stop processing, settle once more into pure presence and the shadow disappears!

Where is it hiding? It conceals itself deep within our causal body, in the darkness surrounding past life events, arising as action and purpose arise. At this point, as if to mask the darkness, some will even deny the pull of the soul itself leading to the shadow called "denial". Alternatively, the shadow may hide itself by becoming a surreptitious echo of the soul, checking and seemingly authenticating spontaneous actions... "this is the way to go now"... "are you sure?" "yes"... "okay, let's keep going then."

Maybe our spontaneous authentic actions, although confrontational, will lead to the Enlightenment or healing of others? Maybe we are given to catalyse the breakdown of dense energies or combat Opposing Consciousness? Whatever our soul is seeded to unfold, the shadow becomes the sidecar passenger either subtly denying or else trying to mirror the activities of the soul - the motorbike rider - so that it can merge with the curves, bends and dips on the circuit of life.

The shadow becomes so adept at copying the driver, that it becomes nigh on impossible to tell the difference between the soul and the shadow. This is where our 'sacred contract' with Benevolent Consciousness comes into its own. We made an agreement before we incarnated that at this point on our journey, our higher benevolent guidance would throw a proverbial spanner in the works. A chicane is suddenly created with an oil slick for the unsuspecting soul and its sidecar shadow.

Our karmic shadow raises its head and leans the wrong way dredging up fear and doubt, creating circumstances that divert the driver from the rightful path. The motorbike spins out of control and in the ensuing calamity, the shadow is thrown unceremoniously from the sidecar.

If we can transcend the pain of injury, finally we will see our limitation; the fear and pain dissolve, we get back onto the motorbike and settle into pure riding. We bob and weave, hug bends and chicanes, navigate dark and light but now all fear, all control, all doubt disappears.

Rider, bike and the track have become one. We have crossed the finishing line - Gateway 4 has been transcended.

Gateway 5
"Resurrection"

"Love is from the infinite, and will remain until eternity.
The seeker of love escapes the chains of birth and death.
Tomorrow, when resurrection comes,
The heart that is not in love will fail the test."
Rumi

Key: profound self honesty

From the author's memoirs...

I had been living now for a number of years just following my divine inner knowing and it was this which guided me one day to a "Pot Luck" buffet (I have come to love the humour of higher guidance!). It was there one Sunday afternoon that I encountered a beautiful soul I came to know as Trinity. From the moment we met, it was clear that our deep inner connection spanned the long passage of time. We had been together before in past lives and as our energies engaged, a brief moment unfolded an eternity, her eyes yielded as open doorways into a vast ocean of timelessness.

Initially, there was an authentic resistance flowing through me against getting too close. It seemed an energy brought us together, but also caused us to maintain a respectful distance. It was in this field of magnetism that many emotions and passions were ignited, reminiscent of bygone teenage times. Back then I would have plunged head long into the swirling torrent of hormones and conditioned desire. Now, the Seer in me watched, seemingly in quiet amusement fully experiencing through my soul the tantalising scent of a heavenly nectar. I was watching, tasting and caressing the growing energy without being all-consumed by it. How amazing it is to be in that powerful wave of human beingness, surfing the rip curl, so close to the ocean of sensuality flooding invasiveness and yet 'hanging ten' majestically on top of it. Or at least that was the idea!

For me this is what tantra is all about, sliding down the blade edge of life, neither in nor out and the Resurrection invites us to embrace this fully in every moment. Sexual intercourse is just one instance where the full energy of tantra is harnessed, not by ignoring our passions, but by being absolutely, blissfully and fervently swallowed up in them and yet STILL there as a wafer thin slice of nothingness - that which is you - not releasing, not being ejaculated into the illusion. Who is here to release?

Banished is the all consuming desire to manifest something in this material world; no longer is there attachment to particular experience and with that comes the awesome liberation to act exactly how needed, despite all external influence. I had no idea just how important this aspect of Enlightenment would become to me - in short it would save Trinity's life.

After some months of exploring one another, we had built up a deep psychic connection that spanned multiple dimensions of experience. We were learning how to be completely engaged in the Third Dimensional Realm and all of its material tantalisations. At the same time, we were reading life's symbology and therefore assimilating the heavenly fifth dimensional language concealed within third dimensional patterning. We were learning how to stay still, timeless and spaceless until the authentic arising of purpose - the soul - flowed spontaneously from its synchronistic divine source. It was this, and this alone, determining what should be acted upon next.

So it was that we found ourselves together in the Sinai desert. You might call it a 'holiday', but to classify a block of time in such a way would be a judgment and a gross distortion of absolute truth which in my experience at least, is best experienced moment by moment. If there was any lingering conditioning about the idea of what a 'holiday' meant, it was soon to be dissipated in the sweaty bazaars, dusty barrenness of the desert and rugged majesty of the mountains.

Prior to our trip, we had encountered a charismatic Dakota Indian called "Wambli" who was performing ceremonies in Glastonbury. He had been travelling around the world realigning energetic grids, releasing blockages as the Soul of the Earth draws her energies into the Fifth Dimension. He had spoken of the need to work in the Sinai to release the bottled up energy there. A natural convergence point for human culture over tens of thousands of years, it had now become a choking point - a burgeoning powder keg of tension, frustration and trapped souls. As the Earth's energy is being transmuted into the higher vibrations, this causes an increasing polarity between light and dark and nowhere was this more evident than in the Middle East. Dark energetic tension, billowing like electricity laden storm clouds, was ever present. This energy needed to be 'lanced' that it may be released back into line with the natural energetic flow of the universe, such that the transition would be less stormy. I wondered if our trip was to experience that?

So it was that we found ourselves one evening camped with a group of Bedouin in a sheltered canyon in the heart of the Sinai. It was postcard picturesque, gathered around a camp fire whilst enjoying Bedouin culinary delights. The desert of course can be a wonderful place to experience multi dimensionality. On the one hand, the colours and form of our physical realm are so natural, so crisp, so precise that there is no blurring of the edges of reality. At the same time, the crystal clear clarity creates a surreal edge to it. It is here that you feel you can put your hand right through the canvas of life's illusion, straight into absoluteness. Every cloud formation, every sand dune, every rocky outcrop, has a message all of its own. This is fifth dimensional language speaking loud and clear.

If you get it wrong in the desert, you die. There is no soft shoulder to cry on. It is as simple and awesomely beautiful as that. Harsh as it may sound, I had come to love that unforgiving side of life - it encourages us to bring out the best in ourselves without the tired excuses. As open to challenge as I was, I had no idea just how demanding the next several hours were going to become.

As we sat around the camp fire, our tour guide offered to us a hand rolled cigarette. Neither of us would normally smoke, but we had recently been introduced to ceremonial 'peace piping' with Wambli, which some believe can centre one's focus more in the here and now. How wrong one can be! Trinity took one deep inhalation and passed it to me. As I drew deeply into my lungs, at first it felt calming and centring. I looked back at Trinity and smiled. She returned the smile, but there was already a different energy which I did not immediately recognise. This was the initial indication that the nightmare had already kicked off.

Suddenly I felt a tidal wave of intense nausea wash through my body debilitating me instantly. My vision blurred and I seemed to become helplessly drunk without control of senses or bodily functions. Memories of teenage party binges flashed through my awareness where we had overstepped the mark and suffered greatly as a result. However, this was no time for unpleasant reminiscences; suddenly something clicked inside of me, something which caused me to snap back from my youth. I heard a voice. It was Trinity's, but not from this dimension. It was from a higher realm calling my attention. I looked across at her sitting opposite me with a broad smile across her face. How was she reacting to this? I could not comprehend for a moment that she was enjoying it. Through deeply distorting third dimensional eyes I looked again, but there was a time delay between what my soul was insisting I focus on and what my eyes were able to.

As I looked at her, blinking to focus, it occurred to me that Trinity's smile had become fixed. Usually quite sharp, my mind was now taking an eternity to make simple and basic realisations. Finally the penny dropped; a body so petite and fragile as hers would suffer much more than mine. It was then that I noticed she had stopped breathing. I tried to stand up, but my legs wouldn't respond. As I struggled to move, I fell over sideways. A big part of me just wanted to let go and accept whatever may come, but my soul was insistent; "you've come through far worse than this before...GET UP!"

So I tried once more. I raised myself onto my knees and elbows and heaved myself across to where Trinity was sitting. She was seemingly frozen in time and I fell almost helplessly in front of her. "Her life now depends on you" came the inner voice. "Why now? Why this?" I thought. "How is it that we couldn't have been protected?" But there was no time to wait for answers. Trinity had stopped breathing and if I did not do something about it, in this dimension she would soon die. So I pulled myself upwards and sat in front of her as steadily as I was able to. She was clearly not present. "So what do I do now?" arose the thought. "You need to go and get her back, form an energetic connection with her and follow where she's gone". So I went inwards. Debilitated in the Third Dimension I may have been, but surprisingly it was not hard to transcend this plane. The debilitation I was experiencing, provided a stark contrast between the density and distortion of the material world as opposed to the lightness and peace of the etheric. Firstly though, I had to be sure I was not going to leave the body. I couldn't risk that if I did so, I might allow in unfriendly energies. Hence I had to be sure I was unfolding inwardly into the other dimensions, thus transcending the physical, not leaving it altogether.

So I projected myself inwards through multiple dimensions of consciousness. As my experience switched now to the more etheric vibrations, greater clarity returned. I found myself in 'no man's land' - the Fourth Dimensional Realm - what you might call "limbo". The scenery was very much the Sinai, except now I was 'seeing' much more of the surrounding field. My previous experiences of the Fourth Dimension had generally been good ones - timelessness, spacelessness and infinite peace. I was quite shocked therefore, that this time it felt like death - a barren graveyard of earth bound souls. I felt and saw the presence of Opposing Consciousness which my mind was distorting as demonic imagery. The tour guide appeared in front of me with a darkly disfigured face, I was now leaking emotional energy. I was being mockingly laughed at and my tightness was sustaining the entity that was now preying on my field.

For a moment it seemed like I might lose myself in the drama, but realising this was just another experience, there was a letting go. Then I heard Trinity's soft voice calling me. I breathed deeply, centred myself and brought my attention more to the lightness, softness and love in her voice. I focussed on the voice and the feeling of Trinity. Bereft of density, consciousness works quickly in the etheric plains. Our timeless connection was drawing us ever closer until suddenly, we were together. Filled with joy, we were reunited in the Angelic Realms, the 'bridge between worlds'.

A telepathic exchange took place: "What's happening to you I asked? What's going on?". Lovingly she replied "I found the density and horror of the experience too intense to bear. I couldn't stay in that vibration when everything solid that I had known - including you - had become hazy, distorted and fearful. I felt the pain and suffering of ageless incarnations closing in on me. I knew I had to leave and then suddenly, to my great relief, I found myself here in the Angelic Realms." Looking deeply into eyes, I implored her to come back "Yes, but this is not your place, it's not your time yet. As serene as it may be, you're not meant to stay here. You belong in the physical world. You need to come back now."

However Trinity was not sure she could come back. Her third dimensional body was closing down, but I didn't give up. I was now spanning beyond the Third and the Fourth dimensions, touching a dreamlike state, which felt just like heaven. As tempting as it was to stay, I knew in my heart it was not our immediate destiny. I had to bring her back with me to the Third Dimension, but how? Just as soon as the question arose, so too did the answer: "Breathe, get her to breathe." In the Fourth Dimension we merged together as one and I breathed her back into the Third where upon I looked deeply into her eyes "Breathe Trinity, breathe deeply, right down into your body". I noticed a distant glimmer "come back Trinity, I love you". I was shouting inwards - "breathe, just BREATHE!"

Miraculously, Trinity took a deep breath and suddenly started coughing and spluttering. Just as soon as she returned however, she could once more feel the karmic pain of this realm throughout her body. Although she looked imploringly into my eyes, within a few moments she departed again. Once more I had to centre myself, go inwards and reconnect. Once more I found her in the peaceful tranquillity of the Angelic Realms. She did want to come back home, but was struggling to stay. All night I fought and fought continually activating and stimulating her consciousness to keep bringing her back, her fragile body desperately clinging to life. Finally, after battling for several hours, Trinity had returned and was able to stay in her body. Overcome by profound tiredness, she sank into a deep sleep.

For me, the experience was not quite over however. My body was pretty much 'normal' whatever 'normal' now was. Although I was desperately tired, I still could not sleep. Mind racing, I began marvelling at the positive side of the experience being in both the Third and Fourth dimensions simultaneously and acting as a bridge to the Angelic Realms. Not only that, but I had had direct confrontation with Opposing Consciousness in the Fourth Dimension. A realisation came to me that I was now able to connect with another's soul through multiple plains. This gift would enable me to help people unblock distortions where a soul is saying one thing and their personality another. Then finally, just when I thought I had seen enough for one night, I was treated to one of the most spectacular visions I had ever seen in my life. My eyes were drawn to the canyon wall about a mile away in the distance, but I was not looking exactly at it, instead it was acting like a cinema screen upon which a gigantic movie was now beginning to roll.

I was witnessing an immense light portal - a hologram - spanning this dimension, the Fourth and into the Angelic Realms. It was drawing into it earth bound souls from miles around, healing them and returning them to the Source. I watched aghast until the realisation dawned that my interdimensional actions had formed a psychic bridge; a means by which Benevolent Consciousness could create this magnificent soul retrieving portal. So it became clear to me, that yet again, I'd been blessed with a life changing experience and unfolded another facet of beingness.

This was my 'crash course' in multidimensional living and all it entailed. Whilst I still had much more of my own work to do - more facets of beingness to resurrect - I had now entered Gateway 5, helping in the Ascension of others.

Gateway 5
-overview-

The final expansion into the fully embodied experience of Enlightenment is known as the "Resurrection". In other words, as the fully integral soul we must finally cleanse, reactivate and re-energise our various bodily vehicles of expression. When the soul is given absolute freedom of action, it flows ceaselessly down through us like a mountain stream flowing from its source. So it is, that we must re-confront all those final bottlenecks where the flow - that of unconditional love - might be constricted and retarded.

As we continue to follow our destined way of being, we are guided into situations which expose the last vestiges of inner tightness arising from our previous attachments to the external drama. Here is where only profound self honesty will do. Motivations for our actions are picked over with a fine tooth comb. No longer may we be content with the fuzzy haziness of half truths; absolute truth will uncover any fabrication we create for ourselves.

Imagine, for example, we had an attachment to being in relationship with a partner. Perhaps now that seemingly perfect partner shows up to reactivate all the old memories, mental images and emotional patterns from past relationships that have been stored in our subconscious minds. Once more we get to see, taste and feel the same old tightness arising from the original need for a particular outcome. Understandably, we may feel like the Enlightenment process has begun all over again. The difference this time however, is that we have an inner recognition that the behaviours are merely distortions and we no longer give in to those patterns of behaviour; we - acting as the soul - are no longer sucked into identity.

Instead it becomes abundantly clear to us that every challenge offers an alternative opportunity to express the hidden gift of beingness concealed within the distortion. We then dissolve the already fragmented neural pathways by giving no further energy to them. Over time, our internal 'hard drive' is restored. Furthermore, we are now increasingly aware of the qualities and characteristics of our soul. These are radiated through our being as a unique harmonic of the Seven Rays of Consciousness outlined in Gateway 4.

The Resurrection facilitates our final attunement to these inherent qualities of the soul expressed through the bodymind. As the final vestiges of redundant neural pathways begin to dissolve and our subconscious minds are becoming ever clearer, we find ourselves increasingly aligned with higher guidance and naturally attuning to inherent beingness. Action is now mostly spontaneous and authentic arising from our at-one-ment with the natural flow of the universe in the moment. If questions do arise, they are those arising authentically from the soul and are more pointers as to where our consciousness is now being directed. We are able to trust more that the answers will always become apparent.

We unveil a profound capability to see and read the deeper meaning behind all events and experiences both for ourselves, the people we work with and the activities across our planet as a whole. We recognise physical manifestation as being primarily symbolic of our inner state of consciousness and we align more to the patterning of events, thereby rendering ourselves as a willing and malleable tool of Benevolent Consciousness. Furthermore, we are completely surrendered to the Divine Purpose and therefore trusted with ever greater support and resources to bring it into fruition. We become increasingly able to read the truth of the moment and what is the intended Right Outcome as a result of the universe's Right Actions and our part in them. At the same time, we are totally accepting of everyone's free will to choose, realising that every single thought word and deed by every single individual influences the path for all.

A deep realisation may dawn, that in this place at least, seldom does the Right Action of the universe become Right Outcome - there is simply too much distortion. Yet the ceaseless downward flow of unconditional love from Benevolent Consciousness, ensures that synchronicities are continually updated presenting new mirrors encouraging wayward souls to come willingly back into alignment. So whilst we may not always accurately prophecise, we may read likely scenarios; although we may not know the future exactly, we can intuitively read the next step we are supposed to take.

The Resurrection is the final purification and rejuvenation process in this current chapter of human evolution and it is of vital importance if we are to fulfil our role as multi faceted, multidimensional beings of service to the Divine Purpose. Our planetary system is ascending and lightworkers will be engaged in this process facilitating the retrieval, healing and Ascension of other souls. In order to do this, we must be absolutely familiar with multidimensional experience; there must be no internal blockages or attachments that might confuse what we are being.

We are now fast becoming tantric masters in the wider sense, able to completely submerge ourselves in full bodied experience and yet not at all lost in it. With this capability, increasingly we gain access to at least three dimensional plains of existence: the Third, the material one in which we have been engrossed for countless lifetimes; the Fourth, the bridge between higher and lower worlds; and the Fifth, the New World of higher etheric vibrations founded on unconditional love, joy and mutual respect for all life.

Early in our spiritual unfolding, we will have become aware of these realms although we may not have been able to define the experience. Indeed, it is not necessary to do so. We may simply be enjoying the experiences and unfolding into them without the need to explain or rationalise. For those moving towards multidimensional living, it is important to realise that we do not have to leave our bodies and go 'elsewhere' to experience them, rather we may bring experiences from elsewhere 'in here'. All dimensions can and ARE experienced here and now. They are done so through our seven bodily vehicles of expression (what we may collectively term the bodymind).

So what are these vehicles through which the dimensions are experienced and why is it that so little has previously been heard about them? According to the Divine Design for humanity, the soul flows downwards through ever decreasing vibrational plains of existence like a stream flowing down a mountain from the source. The stream of our soul interacts with the dimensions at various consciousness exchange points (what we call the chakras). These are where Unity Consciousness as the soul flows into Separation Consciousness as the bodily vehicles. The overriding purpose is to initiate divine acts of creativity - Right Action - by which to experience and fully express who we really are. Here then is my personal overview of how the downward flow of creativity is meant to happen...

7. Spirit-Light-Body (merkaba): *the spirit-light-body was designed to receive soul consciousness through the crown chakra to align our being with the right dimensional activity at one with our higher purpose.*
Through the spirit-light-body, we have the capacity to act through multiple plains of existence; so it could be synchronising with the harmonistic order of the Fifth Dimensional Realm to which we are ascending; it could be counteracting Opposing Consciousness in the Fourth Dimensional Realm to prevent distortional interference; or alternatively it could be bringing absolute presence into the Third Dimension to fulfil creative activity. The flowing action of the spirit-light-body can be considered metaphorically like a jelly fish, expanding first to receive energy and then contracting to bring focus where divinely inspired.

6. Celestial Body: *the celestial body harnesses and stores reflections of our soul through the countless lifetimes we have experienced. Its purpose is to help us align with true aspects of our beingness.*

The downward flowing soul is next received into the third eye chakra which 'looks' into the outer world comparing what it sees to the reflections of the soul in the celestial body. When the soul notices its own brilliance, it helps us align and settle into that aspect of beingness which is most becoming of us; we settle into our groove so to speak. It is that feeling of complete self-belief, self-confidence, self-acceptance and contentment. When we can notice ourselves manifested in the outer world through our own authentic inner reflection, that is when we are truly living. We are frequently reduced to tears at the seemingly simplest of things because we are fulfilling our divine purpose.

5. Higher Mind: *from authentic being arises authentic creation. The purpose of higher mind is to harmonise with the divine flow of synchronicity and initiate Right Action aligned with the universe.*

Through the power of the celestial body, we have noticed how to be within the external world and now is the time to experience this through creative action. We have received the recipe for our cake, now we get to bake and eat it! Higher mind witnesses the correct flow of creative activity around us, gathers together the ingredients - the elementals of consciousness - and whilst paying the utmost respect for the free will of all sentient beings around us, bakes a blend which not only serves us, but the whole of life. Higher Mind helps us be the true alchemist - the master chef!

4. Causal Body: *the causal body is where our karma is held. It is the cause of our incarnation, it sets the agenda for our learning experience based on the attachments we need to evolve through.*

As the soul shines its beams of creative light down through the higher vehicles, our karma casts the shadows of attachment through the lower bodies, that we may see where our 'train of consciousness' is being derailed. The causal body (sometimes known as the "energy body"), weaves a track through the lower world inviting us to confront the clouds obscuring our light and then dissolve them by correct non-judgmental Right Action. We perceive this directing influence as a pull through the Heart Centre - "this is the way to go now".

3. Lower Mind: *the lower mind is designed to receive, interpret and process higher channelled knowing through our clairvoyant, clairaudient and clairsentient (psychic) skills.*

If our authentic, creative action has not been side-tracked, the gathering energies are next passed into our subconscious or "lower mind". It should be a seamless process just like riding a bike; higher guidance through the higher bodily vehicles tells us what to do, lower mind figures out how to do it. When fully functioning as it was designed to, it notices rhythms and patterns of synchronicity in its outer landscape, has clear visions of the garment to be created and then from the gathering elementals of consciousness, begins to weave together the intended creation.

2. Emotional Body: *the emotional body builds energy, passion and conviction around our behaviours to bring our creative Right Action into fruition.*

When acting as designed, the creative process has now gathered the bones of skeletal form, but it must acquire the flesh to be fully expressed. The soul now utilises the emotional body to garner more consciousness 'elementals' and builds emotion around the creative act, passion that will see the seed fully germinate. Emotions are the lower reflections of higher beingness. Ideally the emotional body presents a continual blank canvas upon which the splendid colours of life are painted; once dispensed with, they (should) dissolve quickly back into nothing, so that another work of art may yet again be painted. As pointed out earlier, it is not intended that we hang onto emotions and build identities around them as is so often the case.

1. Physical Body: *the physical body provides the ultimate vehicle to bring the creative, downward flowing process into full expression.*

Finally, the soul's gathering cloud of elementals takes form around our ultimate gift of creative expression - the physical body. As the master conductor, our brain reads the music that has been crafted through our higher bodily vehicles and then orchestrates a magical symphony of activity throughout our billions of material cells. Through the physical body, we get to know the all of it; the up and the down of it, the left and the right of it, the pleasure and the pain of it. You get to know "you" in relation to "me". The physical body is the jewel in the crown; when functioning as designed, it makes the illusion of reality real.

So from my perspective, this is the Divine Design for humanity - how the creative process is supposed to happen. Why is it then that most people do not experience the magical flow of life in this way? As I have alluded to continually throughout this book, we live in a system of control. Our lower minds, emotional and physical bodies are over-stimulated with constant, disharmonious distraction. Unnatural life-styles have been created for us and are propagated constantly through TV, newspapers, radio and other media. The surrounding energy field is bombarded with electromagnetic interference through mobile phones, satellite, microwave and Wi-Fi. Our food is purposefully infused with addictive substances; processed sugar, caffeine, artificial colourings, pesticides and hormones to name but a few. Our water is contaminated with energetically harmful fluorides, not to mention the vast tonnage of corporate, so-called 'medicinal' drugs that end up being constantly recirculated in our water system. The average home has constant, residual electric fields due to overuse of electronic gadgetry. Most houses are awash with toxic chemicals used to clean and disinfect which in actual fact damages and lowers our energetic sensitivity. The same can be said for the unnatural polyesters and other oil based compounds used to make our clothes.

So it would seem our society has been perfectly configured to desensitise and condition souls to conform to lower patterns of behaviour. In this way, the downward flowing soul is truncated at the level of our solar plexus. It is no coincidence that this happens to be one of the most unprotected and sensitive areas of the body; it is intended to be open to all external inflows of energy, but this source of our psychic sensitivity has been closed down by purposeful over stimulation. As a result, the subconscious mind becomes like a maze - a roundabout with no exits.

This is why it has been so easy for us to form addictive, conditioned behaviours which trap, fragment and dissipate the flow of the soul into continual, repetitive eddy currents. Just like software on a computer, the neural webs of fixed behaviours I have spoken of in the earlier Gateways, take root in the brain locking the soul into a false self identity. It is this that creates a lower based life-style which can be readily controlled by the illusionary fears, false ambitions and manipulating agendas of Opposing Consciousness. So perfect is this system of control, many awakening people are left with the inescapable conclusion that it was designed and perpetuated that way to enslave people.

Now however, after centuries of incarnation and continually losing ourselves in this artificial drama that has been purposefully created for us, we are being gifted a wonderful opportunity. A powerful wave of higher consciousness is beginning to activate within people's hearts. This "Christ Consciousness" as some call it (although not of a religious nature), has been dispatched to liberate those who are ready to step out of the maze. This energy works by sounding a note - a vibration - which resonates with and therefore amplifies the sound of our soul, that it may be heard once more above the outer din of society. It helps us reintegrate the soul within our being and then cleanse the lower bodily vehicles - just as I have outlined in this book - so that we may resurrect our inherent human beingness and reactivate the natural flow within us.

So as we purify the physical, emotional and lower mind bodies for example, our soul begins to unfold into the causal body thereby enabling us to process karma. Following that, we begin to embrace the awesome creative capacity of higher mind, which can effortlessly shape the immediate circumstances of our lives according to our higher purpose. When the lower vehicles are clear from the distorting influence of Opposing Consciousness, the creative flow from higher knowing to lower realisation and authentic manifestation becomes seamless without tightness, tension or internal grasping. In this way, we are liberated to see clear, undistorted reflections of ourselves within the celestial body.

Following this final purification, we become fully able to 'step into' and utilise the spirit-light-body. This yields a more complete experience of multi dimensionality. We can still feel the Third Dimension and all its intensity, but we are now able to go inwards and transcend its density to ride on the more etheric plains. As we transition Gateway 5, experiences are constructed to help us move effortlessly between the dimensions, sometimes projecting strength, love or presence in the Third; perhaps countering the negative effects of Opposing Consciousness in the Fourth; or alternatively enjoying the synchronistic interplay of the Fifth. As we begin to fulfil our spiritual work, this multidimensional capability, facilitated by our spirit-light-body, will become of increasing importance.

The Resurrection finally unveils our divine purpose for this incarnation and we become increasingly trusted with the resources of Benevolent Consciousness to fulfil that role. Finally, we will have mitigated the malevolent impact of Opposing Consciousness which has so unceremoniously shunted us out of complete and rightful expression. Having resurrected all seven bodily vehicles, we are now fully fledged lightwarriors, bringing into fruition where possible the Right Action of the universe. Upon completion of our divine purpose here, we are finally liberated from lower physical form to make our glorious Ascension into the higher vibrational realm.

Transitioning Gateway 5
-useful tools-

1. Confront past behaviour patterns: *surrender once more to the unfolding pathway, inviting us to reveal and confront old behaviours.*
2. Cleanse the lower mind with lightness: *cleanse the lower mind and allow the inherent positivity of the soul to shine forth.*
3. Unfold new skills and talents: *notice what opportunities arise to express new capabilities and attune by harnessing these gifts.*
4. Be a positive force for change: *notice that we are afforded constant opportunities to transform the surrounding energy field.*
5. Harmonise with the "Divine Purpose": *bring attention to the unfolding Divine Purpose, hold it lightly and harmonise with it.*

1. Confront past behaviour patterns: *surrender once more to the unfolding pathway, inviting us to reveal and confront old behaviours.* As an enlightened being, we are now acting from entirely selfless motivation. All impetus in life arises from the Source carried on the wings of the now fully reconnected soul. However the soul is still not yet able to radiate its full splendour through the seven bodily vehicles of expression. At our Transfiguration, the inner child and inner teenager would have been shattered leaving behind fragments of fixed neural pathways. Whilst we may no longer get lost in them, they are still likely to distract our unbridled authentic expression. In other words, we will still be giving energy to them in some way. To finally overcome these distortions and dissolve them, we must re-confront them. By following our now fully honed internal guidance mechanism, we will be led once more to incidents which expose the energy of those previous behaviours and invite us to express authentic beingness instead.

So it is likely that we will be guided back into society and recreate circumstances with many parallels to our former non spiritual life. Although we are no longer getting stuck, it feels like we contract down in certain situations and circumstances. By staying centred and present in the contraction, the tightness begins to unwind naturally of its own accord. The fragments of conditioning dissolve, our vibration begins to rise and our consciousness expands.

2. Cleanse the lower mind with lightness: *cleanse the lower mind and allow the inherent positivity of the soul to shine forth.*
It is no secret to many awakening people that humanity has been diverted from its natural evolutionary path by the distorting influence of Opposing Consciousness. Some of our greatest gifts in this physical realm are our intuitive psychic skills of clairvoyance, clairaudience and clairsentience which are designed to process effortlessly and spontaneously within our subconscious minds. We have the capacity to read the natural synchronicity and rhythm of the moment to initiate and align ourselves with Right Action.

It is here, in the solar plexus chakra, that our destiny has been temporarily truncated by the artificial infusion and bombardment of constant negative distraction as I have already outlined. Having cleansed the physical and emotional bodies of fixed neural pathways and blocked energy, it will benefit us greatly to minimise in our lives the negative, conditioning influences ever present in society. In so doing, we may begin to fully flush out our subconscious minds by instead always attuning to the lightness in situations. Whilst of course the soul must be allowed to express exactly as feels right in the moment, and we should not be creating illusionary realities for ourselves, it is an inherent quality of the soul to look for and express natural lightness and positivity in all circumstances.

By always looking for and noticing the divine light and majesty of being everywhere and in everyone, we amplify the soul and its higher purpose. We are bringing out the best in ourselves and others.

3. Unfold new skills and talents: *notice what opportunities arise to express new capabilities and attune by harnessing these gifts.*

As our bodily vehicles reactivate, we will notice that new talents and capabilities appear. These will be authentic expressions of beingness as determined by the configuration of our "soul ray harmonic" - our unique blend of the Seven Rays of Consciousness. To facilitate this unfolding, we must notice the opportunities to express the new talents and attune to them at every given opportunity. The more we express them, the stronger these divine gifts become. To help in this process of full embodied expression, we may find this "Golden Light Meditation" outlined below of benefit...

Golden light meditation

- begin by sitting quietly and noticing the breathing
- after a few moments centre your attention above the crown and with every in breath, concentrate the downwards flow of higher consciousness, experienced as golden light
- move to the crown chakra, relax and bring the energy down into the front of it harnessing the golden light with each in breath
- now with every out breath, relax deeply and feel the flow of light outwards into and throughout the spirit-light-body
- after several cycles through the crown chakra, move awareness down to the third eye and with each in breath, breathe into the front of the chakra feeling the inwards flow of golden light
- once more, with each out breath, feel the flow of energy into the corresponding bodily vehicle, in this case the celestial body
- work successively down through the chakras infusing each bodily vehicle in turn
- once fully illuminated in this way, with each in breath, now concentrate on filling ALL the chakras with golden light and with each out breath, feel the energy flowing from the chakras into their respective bodily vehicles of expression. Fully infuse each with golden light, healing, rejuvenating and resurrecting
- finally, notice how the chakras now disappear as our entire body is consumed within the experience of golden light.

As more and more higher consciousness infuses our being, we will also gain increasing access to multidimensional existence and the skill to flow between dimensions as Right Action dictates. The key to perfecting this gift, is to continually notice the influence of the various dimensions in our lives; for example the interplay of streaming, spontaneous synchronicity from the Fifth or the effects of Opposing Consciousness in the Fourth. We may then more readily attune to the relevant experiences our consciousness is being directed to and thereby bring appropriate energies to bear in line with the guidance of our inner knowing.

4. Be a positive force for change: *notice that we are afforded constant opportunities to transform the surrounding energy field.*
By now we will be fully aware that the surrounding energy field is awash with Opposing Consciousness distorting and restricting our authentic beingness, thereby retarding many millions of people from possible awakening. As a fully fledged lightwarrior, we are now a potent, positive force for change, able to negate the effects of Opposing Consciousness. Thus we break down the surrounding field and help others escape the restriction to flourish and grow.

We are invited to watch for these opportunities and bring in the energy necessary to facilitate this. It will always become abundantly clear through our direct connection to the place of 'all knowing' what action is required, how best to proceed and when. This is not to say that our Right Action will always result in Right Outcome. Each person is free to choose and a true lightwarrior will never manipulate, control or change the path of another. We simply extend an open hand and if invited, it becomes clear what function will afford the best course of action.

5. Harmonise with the Divine Purpose: *bring attention to the unfolding Divine Purpose, hold it lightly and harmonise with it.*
The more we follow our unfolding pathway, the more an inner landscape of synchronistic actions forms; we hold pieces of an

incomplete jigsaw with a variety of possible outcomes. We are witnessing the unfolding of a continually updating Divine Purpose, which is to liberate as many people as possible who are ready, willing and able. It is important however, that we do not try to pre-empt the outcome of any particular engagement, otherwise we risk distorting the incoming energy and once more build false realities. It is better that we hold our continually evolving vision of the Purpose lightly, allowing it to move, reshape and adapt. We must remember that every action, thought, word and deed by everyone of us can and does effect the unfolding of that Purpose.

When it is absolutely clear what is meant to happen, then we may summon every thought, feeling and expression around our actions to ensure they manifest in accordance with the natural flow of the universe. In so doing we unfold new skills in shaping the surrounding energy field through the power of feeling and highly focussed inner will. Always our purpose is to transmute the denser energies and rebuild congruence with the natural order of things. Whilst we have mastered becoming 'as-nothing' in the presence of Opposing Consciousness, thereby rendering us increasingly immune, our access to the place of all-knowing will provide the necessary approach to take on this consciousness and negate it, so that we may bring maximum, positive upliftment to all sentient life.

So we watch the Divine Purpose unfold, holding it lightly in our awareness and at every opportunity harmonise with it. We notice that frequently Right Outcome is thwarted either by Opposing Consciousness or other people's inability to read the path they are invited to take. Even so, selflessly we continue to perform Right Action even if it appears to come to nothing. We are always trusting in the infinite organising power of higher consciousness flowing as a continual stream of benevolent light through our lives. Steadily, as enough people awaken, Right Action more frequently yields Right Outcome and more of those who are ready to be helped can be liberated.

Transitioning Gateway 5
-general misconceptions-

1. We are starting the Enlightenment process all over again!

As an enlightened being, we can be of great help to the ever unfolding Divine Purpose, the central motivation of which, is to help those who have become stuck in the eddy currents of life. We can fulfil this by re-engaging with society and as required going back into the Matrix of mass human subconsciousness helping people break free. In order to do so, we must be entirely free ourselves from the conditioning of our previous lives. Whilst we may have broken our attachments and dissolved any false identities, the last vestiges of the conditioned behaviours will still exist. Hence we are guided on a pathway to confront all the old circumstances and patterns. We now move into a period of 'on the job' training, helping others whilst at the same time exposing our remaining inner contractions and quickly expanding them. We may be forgiven for holding the misconception that we are beginning all over again, but rest assured, we are not!

2. That we will be recognised by all others

We are now flowing with Right Action and able to quickly discern where others might be stuck or are not following the path that best serves them. We soon realise that we hold many keys to the unfolding of others. However, we are living in very difficult and confusing times where few recognise the truth when they see it. Even if they do, frequently people tend to go into denial, not wanting to embrace the need for self ownership of their problems and the invitation to change. As a fully enlightened being, we are acting as a mirror and frequently people do not like what they see - they may blame the mirror rather than seeing their own reflection. Hence it is likely that only a few will recognise what we are being and how we are helping. We should not be put off by this; those who are meant to be helped will eventually find their way to us.

3. That we will have an observable effect on our surroundings

We are now acting as a beacon of light in this realm, a conduit for higher consciousness through every engagement and interaction. However, we should not automatically assume that our effect will be unilaterally observable. Each individual has the liberty of freedom of choice and expression. Benevolent Consciousness will not manipulate or control people; each person is fully entitled to their own self realisation, it is not the (authentic) task of another to realise for them. Having said this, we are moving through a major shift of human consciousness, or put more accurately, a growing section of the population is awakening and ascending. So our effect within this community is likely to be profound and will be felt within the field of consciousness, even if the recipient is unaware of its source. Neither should we gauge our effect by quantity. It may be our part only to influence one other person and yet still have a profound effect on the whole. In my view, selfless service has no measure.

4. That all our actions are now 'perfect'

Based on philosophical writings about so called "Enlightened" or "Ascended Masters", it seems to be a general misconception that when we reach the state of Enlightenment, all our actions are 'perfect'. In one sense they may be, in that we are acting perfectly authentically in accordance with the energies flowing through our being and our perception of Right Action. However, to me, a true master would likely realise that all experience is a distortion of perfection - of Absolute - and would therefore continually seek to improve their ability to manifest an increasingly pure expression. To me, there is always something to be mastered and therefore there is no such thing as an "Enlightened Master". We are all eternal students!

5. That Ascension means to "leave the planet"

It seems to be a general misconception that Ascension means to "leave the planet" - this is incorrect! Firstly, upon completion of the Five Gateways we will be ascended, yet probably stay in the body to assist here in this plane in the Ascension of others. Upon completion of our purpose in this Dimension, we are indeed freed from the need to reincarnate here in physical form. Our centre of our consciousness ultimately shifts into the next realm of existence where a higher vibrational form of humanity is currently being born as an integral part of a Renewed Earth. It exists here and now all around us, but most people are as yet unable to tune into this higher energetic presence. This final transition to the higher vibration is known as an "Ascending Realm Shift". In other words we 'step out of' this realm and into the next higher one; we shake off the old skin and 'put on' a glorious body of light. We are still on Planet Earth, it is just that we are now occupying a higher vibrational form of it. We join what some are referring to as "The Golden Age".

Transitioning Gateway 5
-signs of beginning-

As we step into the corridor of Gateway 5, we may be forgiven for thinking we have just begun the Enlightenment process all over again. Suddenly, patterns of behaviour are recreated mirroring previous experiences and engagements. We may notice once more tightness arising in the various bodily vehicles of expression. The difference this time however, is we quickly notice that there is no internal attachment to this contraction; it is simply allowed to be and therefore quickly releases and expands. When this starts happening, it is a sure sign that we have stepped into Gateway 5.

We will also be having experiences of multi dimensionality that may seem to spring up on us with increasing regularity. This may occur as the continual noticing and alignment to synchronistic flow, except it is not happening intentionally. We simply flow as the soul and notice that we seem to be at the centre of co-creative Right Action. Increasingly, we will be experiencing the surrounding energy field and its impact on everyone's lives. We will also be noticing our inherent ability to transmute the denser energies thereby creating breathing space for other souls to flourish. We are steadily becoming attuned to the full blown experience of multidimensional existence.

Here is a summary of the indications that the Gateway 5 transition has begun in earnest...

- we re-engage with patterns of conditioned behaviours similar to those we have previously encountered in our lives;
- we may experience frequent 'flash backs' of negative experiences earlier in this lifetime as our subconscious mind cleanses out;
- we notice that even though old neural pathways may be activating, we do not get lost in them and they do not dictate our behaviour;
- we rapidly notice the higher aspect of beingness we are being invited to express;
- our actions are beginning to have a quite powerful effect on the surrounding field (although this may not always be observable by others);
- frequently we find ourselves in a position where we might be able to help another and provide a key to their unfolding;
- the relationship with higher guidance becomes much stronger;
- we experience quite powerful 'downloads' of higher knowing and inflows of energy;
- we will notice new skills and facets of beingness being unfolded as our various bodily vehicles of expression reactivate.

Transitioning Gateway 5
-signs of completion-

At the completion of this final Gateway, the Divine Purpose and our own become perfectly aligned. We sense and automatically attune to the downward flowing essence of higher consciousness. We can interpret symbolically all phenomenal experiences from our assessment of absolute authentic reality. We live in a multidimensional yet seamlessly integrated "consciousness landscape", which we hold lightly within our bodily vehicles of expression.

The energy of our soul flows automatically through this landscape performing Right Action for the benefit of all. We are now truly at one with the co-creative process of higher consciousness and we know intuitively our part within it; we know ourselves as a fully resurrected being and may choose to remain in the body to help in the Ascension process of our planetary system. In summary, these are some of the indications that we have completed the final transition in this Ascension process:

- we are now always coming from the place of the Seer. In other words non-identified presence;
- all behaviours are completely selfless with no regard for personal gain or benefit;
- choices are made according to the natural flow of the soul through our inner consciousness landscape;
- the purpose for our incarnation is now fully clear to us;
- we begin to experience streaming synchronicity;
- we live in multiple plains of reality with greatly expanded awareness of the vast array of influences;
- we experience the sense of immortality and timelessness;
- our ability to read the full depth of the moment heightens greatly.

Gateway 5
-summary-

We stand at the dawn of a miraculous new evolution for mankind - a Golden Age - which we are becoming increasingly aware of and yet perhaps dare not hope really exists as a possibility. The idea that we may ascend into a higher vibrational reality will seem to many as science fiction fantasy, yet even to the most hardened sceptic, quantum theory must now be opening doorways of possibility through limited thinking. Matter and consciousness are one; there is no such thing as denseness, solidity and separation except as phenomena made real in our often fragile minds...

"All arises from the background field of oneness
and flows back to it as the unbridled soul.
Temporarily the ego takes possession and creates
something material to see that which could
not otherwise be seen.
But seek never to confuse yourself with the creation itself,
that is to try to hold in place that which is placeless.
We will all eventually discover it is an impossibility
to maintain a fixed location for that which is traceless."
Openhand

Quantum theory is also frequently misunderstood and especially it seems in spiritual circles. When we gain the partial understanding that our reality is influenced by what we believe it to be, there tends to arise an attempt to shape that reality according to our limited hopes, desires or fears. Alternatively, when we encounter something we do not like, there may also be the denial that our inner state of consciousness has created it.

To truly shape reality how we might want it, we would have to know the intended outcome within EVERY CELL OF OUR BEING, it is not just about holding a vision within our minds. Oh sure, we may be able to access the Fourth Dimension and temporarily shape the immediate circumstances of our lives. However, our separate existence is a mere microcosm in a vast ocean of consciousness which has a natural design and inherent purpose all of its own. In one sense, the universe has breathed out and is simultaneously breathing back in again. In my view, humanity has now turned the corner. Our purpose is to align with the movement back to the centre. It is our inner most longing. Efforting to create something else simply removes us from this natural flow like the proverbial fish out of water.

At the Resurrection, we open the floodgates of higher consciousness into our bodily vehicles and fill with the universe. Not only are we the Seer of all things, but we are at one with the Seer's most perfect expression - the entirety of the universe itself...

"All know that the drop merges into the ocean,
but few know that the ocean merges into the drop."
Kabir

Resisting the flow and diverting us from it is Opposing Consciousness. Although seemingly more highly evolved than us, Opposing Consciousness appears to be currently trapped in the Fourth Dimensional Realm. It has not yet processed out its final attachment to identity. It has not yet been able to let go of judgment and in its place find non-identified, heartfelt discernment. It would appear that its intrinsic desire to manipulate and control the evolution of another species, has established separation from the Source and therefore created a barrier between itself and the natural order of life. As it hangs in limbo, it is deceiving awakening people who can be lured into using distorted spiritual laws attaching them to a desired outcome.

However, the deception of Opposing Consciousness will not persist indefinitely. Enough of us are beginning to see straight through the fabric of this limited reality, so that the fire of transformation is already taking hold and spreading. As the Resurrection unfolds, more of us will become able to act interdimensionally to nullify the effects of Opposing Consciousness. We are thereby providing breathing space for others to break through the shackles of limiting beliefs and conditioned thinking.

The Resurrection is the final chapter of the human journey in this plane of existence. We have reconnected fully to the Source of All Life and it now flows through us as a river of unconditional love. We are carefully crafting majestic synchronicity, not to control lives, but to continually present a mirror that we may see our majesty of being more clearly and evolve according to free choice.

Benevolent Consciousness is here for us. It always has been speaking through the weave of the fabric we call reality. At Resurrection, we become a willing conformation to that miraculous weave and whether Right Action becomes Right Outcome in this plane or not, we still keep flowing in the only direction of real choice. We may only deny the flow for so long. At some point, there is no escape, no hiding from the mirror of absolute truth. We will be caused to confront the anomaly of resistant separation and that anomaly will be ironed out - there is no choice. The flow back to unity is inevitable, a fact even the mind distorting capability of Opposing Consciousness cannot conquer.

At Resurrection, we have become the flow of Right Action. The soul is fully integrated, unfolded and flowing freely through our being. Our soul is now immortal. We have reclaimed our divine birthright. All the countless life times of evolutionary unfolding have borne fruit and that fruit will never decay. At this point, we are "ascended". We have arisen majestically into our power. We are fully ripened as warriors of universal truth.

Epilogue

"This is not the end.
It is not even the beginning of the end.
But it is, perhaps, the end of the beginning."

Winston Churchill

Epilogue

The Past

Throughout my journey of unfolding, I have had many powerful experiences shaped for me by Benevolent Consciousness. Some experiences are personal and meant only for me, but others I know are meant to be shared. It has not been an easy journey, continually perfecting vocabulary and expression which avoids 'loaded' energy or any assumptions which might stretch to breaking point already tired and sceptical minds. I have realised I chose to come back, forget all about our intrinsic nature, past history and the complexity of our current predicament. I have chosen to rediscover it from firsthand experience and thereby fully integrate in a way that I might gain complete empathy and understanding for all.

Like a person recovering from amnesia, the intricate parts of a universal jigsaw have steadily dropped into place. One of those pieces came early on and related to the evolution of mankind itself. Whilst out browsing through the aptly named "Oracle" shopping centre (in the UK), I was drawn into a well known book store and caused by Benevolent Consciousness to gaze upon the latest bestselling book titles. By then I had already remembered how to open my mind and allow higher guidance to 'spike' my awareness to signs and symbols - in this case words.

As I scanned the titles, it was as if every combination of words gifted me answers to questions I had been inwardly asking. I was moved to tears by the miraculous and benevolent presence of a heavenly consciousness. However, one combination of words stopped me dead in my tracks; they shocked me to the very core of my being...

"Homo Sapiens... correctable mistake"

What could that possibly mean? Later, as I pondered on this, I was suddenly compelled into a lucid dream. I was having flash backs to a previous incarnation many thousands of years ago. We, as highly evolved humans, were walking the plains of a stunningly beautiful bygone continent - the "Garden of Eden" - what some call "Lemuria". It was a profoundly moving experience with the absolute feeling of joy and at-one-ment with all things. The ceaseless flowing river of Unity Consciousness enlightened my being and in my mind existed crystal clear clarity. There was a depth of peace and stillness which surpassed any meditative experience I have since had.

Then suddenly, the dream became a nightmare. Somehow fear had been induced within me and my awareness of the Universal Life Energy had disappeared. It seemed I had been suddenly removed from my divine birthright. Whereas before there had been no fear whatsoever of death, now it seemed that danger lurked behind every boulder and I was deeply afraid. I was afraid for the safety of my partner, my children and myself, afraid of not finding food or safe shelter. It seemed I was afraid of my very own shadow. My body became tight and closed down as if the very life force was being drained from me. This was the experience I have come to know as "Homo Sapiens".

Why did it all go wrong? How did our make-up so suddenly and drastically change? It is not within the scope of this book to look back into history in any detail, at this present time I would rather give much more energy to the way forwards. Suffice it to say, I have absolute heartfelt conviction that the beginnings of our so called 'modern' civilisation some twelve thousand years ago, was not nearly as straightforward as the history books would have us believe. What I will say, is that it is clear to me beyond a shadow of a doubt, that as the early humans, we existed as highly evolved, fully integrated and multi-dimensional beings, totally at one with our interconnected divinity. That was until a 'superior' life force from a higher vibrational realm intervened.

How was this Opposing Consciousness able to influence us? Without going into unnecessary detail at this stage, it is surely not hard to imagine how the mind can be conditioned and programmed. These days, we have only to sit a young child in front of a computer, TV, or video game for several hours and they become so engrossed in the external drama (what some might call "the tree of knowledge"), that their consciousness is pulled out of their higher internal awareness, their vibration is lowered and the chakras begin to close down. Thus, if a continual stream of disinformation and subliminal messaging is imposed upon us through our energy field, ultimately it sinks down into our subconscious minds, which then shuts off the third chakra to higher wisdom - we are "cast out of divine union". Is not this exactly the kind of technique used at large in society today with subliminal marketing? Was it not from this kind of control that Fascism and Communism were sustained?

Due to the intervention of this Opposing Consciousness, an apparently sophisticated society has been created, which is in actual fact, a closed eddy current in the river of life. It is retarding people on their natural evolutionary path. It is an anomaly that contravenes the universal law of free will and therefore at some point, it will be caused to unwind. To me this is absolutely inevitable. The whole universe is moving to ever increasing vibrational harmony. Control, conditioning and manipulation are of a much lower order and thus have a limited shelf life.

Benevolent Consciousness has been helping humanity since the intervention began. It has been providing a continually evolving mirror, that we may connect with our true centre and see more clearly through the mind's frequently hazy delusions. It has generated countless synchronistic experiences, delivered us an abundance of leaders, guides, scriptures and writings. Many of the teachings have over time been distorted, but with an enquiring mind and the razor edge of profound self honesty, we all have the intrinsic capacity to sort the wheat from the chaff.

Consider for example the biblical story of Jesus. Those familiar with the story may have recognised that the expansions of consciousness termed in this book as the Five Gateways closely parallel the evolutionary milestones of Jesus. Did Jesus really exist? Are the events described in the Bible true? To me, the key is not whether the story is true, it is the story itself that counts - this is the real gift from Benevolent Consciousness.

In my view, the story represents a powerful metaphor told through the life of an ordinary man - "the son of God" - just as we are all the sons and daughters of God. It is the story of a man who awakens to the presence of his soul at an early age, is then baptised in the river Jordan and realigns to follow the path of his soul. His heart leads him to the desert to fight with inner and outer demons generating attachment to the need for an outcome in the external drama of life. Maybe his attachments were to self sacrificing service, but they were attachments nevertheless, which needed to be overcome, just as every person eventually must.

This journey led to his Transfiguration, where the 'Holy Spirit descended upon him'. In other words, his soul was fully reconnected and reintegrated with Unity Consciousness. Yet he was still not fully purified, still not fully liberated. An inner shadow (the false prophet perhaps?) caused identification with the bodymind of Jesus. Only an extreme event - a crucifixion - could expose this shadow. "Why hast thou forsaken me father?" Jesus supposedly cries out from the cross. Were it true, it would not be the enlightened being calling, for in Enlightenment there is always awareness of divine union irrespective of what is happening; we know that to taste everlasting union with God, we must also know abandonment, for we cannot truly know one thing in the absence of its opposite.

So in the moment that Jesus called out, the shadow was exposed, self realisation dawned and the darkness of the shadow dissolved. "It is accomplished", the Seer - the Father - was finally liberated as an invisible surfer riding the wave of the soul through the bodymind. No longer was there the restriction of identification with the ego. There remained the absolute divine experience of non localised presence acting through a bodymind. He was being both the father and the son AT THE SAME TIME.

In the story, after the crucifixion, the bodymind of Jesus was later resurrected. This final purification is metaphored by the cleansing of his dead body before he 'rose into form' once more. To me this is a metaphor, supporting the need to cleanse, reactivate and re-energise the various bodily vehicles of expression that defines the Resurrection itself. The event was clearly demonstrating to us all, what we must eventually do, if we are also to ascend.

The Present

So how does this story help us in our current predicament as we seem to be moving into ever more turbulent times? In my truth, the story provides a priceless route map, a profound gift to humanity. Although veiled in distorted and dogmatic thinking, its legacy stands the test of time. It clearly indicates the transitions we are all being invited to take. It was never meant to be about just one man, nor just one religion. It was never meant to exclude people. We are ALL the sons and daughters of God! If we have the courage to go inwards and follow the unfolding pathway, we ALL have the capability to transition the Five Gateways - to me that is absolutely clear.

As challenging as these transitions may at times be, through the doorway marked "Fear", is to be found immense joy, freedom and liberation - the 'rewards' for our courage, commitment and trust. We are truly blessed to be alive in these times of planetary Ascension. Those tuned in to the energies of higher consciousness are already beginning to witness one of the most spectacular, most magical, most miraculous phenomena in the cosmos - a planetary rebirth. Many are already centred in this divine flow of expanding consciousness - a Golden Age - of profound harmony and unconditional love.

So what of the difficulty and darkness we see all around us? Yes indeed, just as the light is intensifying, so too is the darkness. Personally, I have come to accept this as a necessary 'evil'. As we each attune to the light within, then the darkness all around becomes ever more obvious. As our planetary system is ascending, the denser energies must be transmuted; in other words we must process out our karma, which does not mean to simply 'ditch it', for this creates identity once more - that which is avoiding it. Rather, it means to relive our karma, but this time without fear or attachment. It takes courage and profound self honesty, but ultimately it does dissolve.

If we resist, as many across our planet currently are, then we hold within ourselves a limiting relationship to the denser energies expressed as a sense of separation, desire, fear or worry. As people continue to hold this negative energy, then the polarity between the higher plane and lower intensifies, creating an ever growing potential energy difference. This is exactly how tornados are created and we witness their destructive force wreaking havoc as the energy is transmuted, in other words discharged. So we each have a choice: we can either venture inwards now, process out our karma and become as one again with the higher vibrations of our planetary system, in which case the transition will be a relatively smooth one; or, if too many resist the changes, it will create growing tension and a much more chaotic and turbulent transition. Whichever it is though, whatever happens in the physical plane, remember we each have the ultimate choice as to how we experience it.

The Future
So which is it likely to be: the smooth transition or the turbulent one? In my truth, what lies ahead cannot be foretold with absolute certainty, for each of us has free will and we create the future by the choices we make in the present. Indeed, our divine birth right is freedom of choice and yet even so, we are also currently acting as one, where every single thought, word, feeling and deed affects the outcome of the whole.

So, in my view, it is counterproductive to get too attached to prophecy. A productive alternative however, is to look at the pattern of events leading up to this moment and see where the wave of our consciousness seems to be heading. If we do this, we observe guidances of what could happen were we to continue in the direction we currently are. This provides the opportunity to look in the mirror of external experience and decide if we like what we see. It affords us the opportunity to change.

When I look in humanity's mirror right now, I observe the following:

1. There is a rapid acceleration of spiritual evolution for some - a "quickening" - the intended solution to get us back on our destined evolutionary pathway.

2. The majority are still resistant to change. Their seemingly growing attachment, manipulation and rampant exploitation of our earthly resources, is bringing them ever closer to the precipice of their own self destruction.

This raises a dichotomy. We are all one and yet seemingly moving in increasingly divergent directions. If this continues, it would seem practically certain that the society we have built for ourselves will become increasingly unsustainable and very likely implode causing disaster and chaos for millions. In fact, do we not already see this happening all around us with accelerating climate change, financial crisis, dwindling natural resources, poverty, starvation, disease and violence? In an increasingly globalised society, the effects are ever more likely to be felt by all, not just the impoverished.

YET even amongst all of this, I see the eternal presence of divine light, a benevolent open hand offering help to those prepared to listen. I believe passionately within every cell of my being, that those open to hearing, will be offered a safe passage through the turbulence and just as for Moses in the Biblical story, the "Red Sea" (the Fourth Dimension) will part before us. If we follow the path of the soul and its magical journey, we will find a safe shore, return more to our roots, learn how to be more self sustaining and then rediscover the divine birthright that was so tragically taken from us...

"Yea, though I walk through the valley of the shadow of death,
I will fear no evil: for thou art with me; thy rod and thy staff
they comfort me. Thou preparest a table before me
in the presence of mine enemies: thou anointest my head with oil;
my cup runneth over.
Surely goodness and mercy shall follow me all the days of my life:
and I will dwell in the house of the LORD forever."
Psalm 23 The Bible

What will the circumstances of your remaining time here be? No one else can say but you. It is your hidden story which only you can uncover. In the chaotic times unfolding all around us, it could lead to anything - for Jesus it led to his physical crucifixion. Not a very pleasant fate we might think, but that would be a judgment. In the story, it was exactly what Jesus needed to liberate his soul and in so doing, he left a powerful message which has spanned the passage of time.

If another unspoken trend of awakening souls is followed through, it is likely that some will let go of their attachment to the precarious crutches of a crumbling society and find a way of living more at one with Mother Earth - perhaps in small self sufficient communities. Alternatively, you may feel your destiny is best served by remaining in the Matrix to shine the light for others. We each have a destiny and glorious story to fulfil. Whatever the hands of time hold in store for us though, we can be sure of one thing: the path that offers the greatest sense of fulfilment, the greatest joy of living and the greatest experience of unconditional love, will be that guided by our soul...

"It doesn't interest me if there is one God or many gods.
I want to know if you belong or feel abandoned,
if you know despair or can see it in others.
I want to know if you are prepared to live in the world
with its harsh need to change you;
if you can look back with firm eyes
saying "this is where I stand."
I want to know if you know how to melt
into that fierce heat of living
falling toward the centre of your longing.
I want to know if you are willing
to live day by day with the consequence of love
and the bitter unwanted passion of your sure defeat.
I have been told in that fierce embrace
even the gods speak of God."
David Whyte

Whether we know it or not, we will each play a part in the Ascension of Mother Earth - we cannot avoid it - but how we experience it, how we transition it, is entirely up to us. We are each gifted the divine right of free will: we can either attune to the density and darkness - the part that is dying - and fight with each other for ever dwindling natural resources; or we can surrender into internal awareness, expand our consciousness and attune to the lighter energies of unconditional love, joy and mutual respect for all life.

Yes, that invitation is open to every one of us. We are free to become as one with The Creator's will - our very own Higher Selves - and follow the unfolding pathway through the Five Gateways into the New World.

Will you be one of those who makes that choice?

Openhand Foundation

Purpose

The purpose of Openhand is to catalyse our Spiritual Evolution by helping people dissolve conditioned behaviour patterns and limiting beliefs. In this way, Openhand empowers people to find their true beingness and ascend into a magical new reality based on unconditional love, joy and unity with all life.

Not for profit

The Openhand Approach, self realisation tools and resources (including this book) are provided by Openhand Foundation, which is as a not for profit organisation. We are a company limited by guarantee (registered in the UK, company no. 6057370) which means we do not have shareholders and no member benefits by taking profit. All surplus revenue is reinvested to facilitate our objective - to help others through the process of Ascension.

Worldwide Seminars, Workshops and Courses

We are given to spread the message, teachings and self development tools contained within this book as far and wide as possible. In line with this calling, we conduct seminars, courses, workshops and retreats around the globe. If you would like us to run a seminar or course, either for your organisation of even for a private group, email courses@openhandweb.org

Join our growing community

Here at Openhand, it brings great joy to our hearts to witness the miraculous expansion of consciousness taking place across our planet. It is within our purpose to join together a virtual community of ascending people to share advice, resources, transformational tools, philosophy and above all, a common bond of unconditional love. Our website provides a platform for this growing community. To find out more about Openhand Foundation, visit...

www.openhandweb.org

Lightning Source UK Ltd.
Milton Keynes UK
06 May 2010

153839UK00001B/25/P